For "Brother Cliff"
Brother clergy.
Brother golfer.

John

Golf
In The
Real Kingdom

A Spiritual Metaphor For
Life In The Modern World

Robert R. Kopp

CSS Publishing Company, Inc., Lima, Ohio

GOLF IN THE *REAL* KINGDOM

Copyright © 2000 by
CSS Publishing Company, Inc.
Lima, Ohio

Library of Congress Cataloging-in-Publication Data

Kopp, Robert R., 1952-
 Golf in the real kingdom : a spiritual metaphor for life in the modern world / Robert R. Kopp.
  p. cm.
 Includes bibliographical references.
  ISBN 0-7880-1580-X (pbk. : alk. paper)
  1. Golfers — Religious life. 2. Christian life — Presbyterian authors. 3. Golf — Religious aspects — Christianity. I. Title.
BV4596.G64 K67   2000
252— dc21   99-055455

This book is available in the following formats, listed by ISBN:
    0-7880-1580-X Book
    0-7880-1581-8 Disk
    0-7880-1582-6 Sermon Prep

PRINTED IN U.S.A.

*To my dad
who
introduced me
to a game
and
taught by example!*

Table Of Contents

Preface

I get up most mornings a little before 4 a.m. I go to the church, make some coffee, do some administrative stuff, and then leave for Dogwood Hills Golf Course in Claysville, Pennsylvania, a little after 5 a.m. We — *there are others* — usually tee off just before the break of dawn, hole out after nine before 7:30 a.m., and then face the day with renewed peace and calm.

I don't even need an alarm to wake up. I always beat the clock by at least fifteen minutes. And if you think that's crazy or why I can empathize with heroin addicts, I know you don't play golf or another *recreational* sport. Ben Hogan said it for us, "I have loved playing the game and practicing it ... I couldn't wait for the sun to come up so that I could get out on the course again."

But the following pages aren't really about golf. They're about surviving the meanness, madness, and misery of life in the modern world *with a smile*. They're about finding a therapeutic distraction that provides a mental bath. For many of you, golf will be a synonym for bowling, bridge, knitting, tennis, biking, hiking, jogging, or whatever. So fill in your word and Will Rogers will make sense: "I guess there is nothing that will get your mind off everything like golf. I have never been depressed enough to take up the game but they say you get so sore at yourself you forget to hate your enemies."

I play golf.

No, I *experience* golf.

Or as Arnold Palmer explained for us, "What other people find in poetry or art museums, I find in the flight of a good drive: the white ball sailing up into the blue sky, reaching its apex, falling and finally dropping to the turf ... just the way I planned it."

Maybe not always the way I planned it.

All I know is something spiritual happens when I'm on the course. I lose my polemical edge. I become irenic. I feel close to

God. Indeed, I talk to God when I play, and not just about the last missed putt.

Golf is a mirror for my soul. It's been said golf doesn't build character. It *reveals* character. I agree. Ken Blanchard is right: "You learn a lot about yourself from golf. I guarantee if you cheat or blow up when you get a bad break or make a mistake, that behavior will show up in other parts of your life. If you maintain a positive attitude in golf, even when things are going sour, I bet that will carry over to other things too" (*Playing the Great Game of Golf*, 1992).

Again, it doesn't have to be golf. As Don Carter suggested, for example, "One of the advantages bowling has over golf is that you very seldom lose a bowling ball."

But everybody needs something.

Golf isn't the most important thing in my life. It runs a distant third behind my Lord and family. But it is important to my life and I thank God for creating it.

In Michael Murphy's *Golf in the Kingdom* (1972), Adam says, "Golf is played on many levels." As Murphy's book mystically explores, golf is played on emotional, intellectual, spiritual, and physical planes.

What follows is my understanding of golf as a metaphor for life even as it provides a therapeutic distraction from life while teaching lessons that apply to life.

Fore!

The First Hole

Awe came upon everyone....   — Acts 2:43

I grew up in the Forty Fort United Presbyterian Church near Wilkes-Barre, Pennsylvania. Though the church has been around for over 200 years, I'm its only son who became a pastor. They even have a picture of me hanging near the back door under an exit sign. Despite my mom's assurances, I've always wondered why it ended up there.

That suspicion aside, Forty Fort U-P did more than any other in shaping my life and ministry. That's where I met Jesus, kissed a girl for the first time (*I always liked youth group*!), received a call to ministry, learned the church *at its best* is about loving like Jesus (invitationally, inclusively, and unconditionally), and met the most influential woman and man of my adolescent years.

Grace Blanchard was 104 when she stopped teaching Sunday school.

Maybe that's why I'm not especially sympathetic when our most seasoned members cite age for begging off boards, committees, and so on. Besides, the tired, tested, and true always have a lot more to offer than ecclesiastical rookies. That's why our pastor emeritus continues to be so vital to us. It takes a long time for theory to catch up with practice.

Anyway, Miss Blanchard had just crossed the century mark when I showed up in her class with nine other boys. She only taught boys. Whenever we asked why, she'd say something about focus. Like most eighth graders, I knew she was wrong. Now I know she was right because I've got one.

The last Sunday of every month was *S-O-S Sunday* in her class — *same old stuff*! Starting in Genesis, she'd review salvation history in a well-drilled Q & A.

During my second year in seminary, she died. Her will dictated that anyone from Forty Fort U-P in seminary was to receive 1,000 dollars from her estate. Appropriately, I used the money to

9

buy books about the Bible. They're in my study. She's in my heart. And the greatest lesson from her remains life in the Lord is perpetually fresh and exhilarating.

I was going to say the Reverend Harold F. Mante was my pastor for over two decades. But, in fact, he'll be my pastor forever. He was my pastor during confirmation class, God and Country Award, high school, college, seminary, graduate school, and right through my ordination on May 8, 1977. He also hung with me through some delinquent moments that would even make my eighth grader blush.

I'll never forget playing golf with my dad and Reverend Mante for the first time. I was about fourteen or fifteen. I striped my tee shot on the first hole right down the middle of the fairway about 250 yards or so. I was pumped, psyched, and ready to assume my destiny as the precursor to Tiger Woods until Reverend Mante flipped another ball to me and challenged, "Let's see if you can do it again."

The first shot was so good.

And I'll never forget the worship service that included my ordination. Reverend Mante preached. He kept pounding away at what he called the three B's of successful life and ministry: Be slow! Be steady! Be solid!

Over two decades later, I cannot get those three B's out of my mind. Whether it's planning church strategy or facing the first tee, it's how I approach just about everything.

Reverend Mante gave me a Princeton Seminary chair to celebrate my ordination. I keep it in my study. I sit on it for meetings and during counseling. It helps me to remember the two greatest lessons taught to me by my pastor. First, unconditionally love people no matter how weird or wily — and I recall how he loved me when I fit into both categories. Second, just like golf, life is more than the first hole and there's always room for redemption, but it's a lot easier if you give it your best shot at the start.

So I approach my vocation (ministry) and avocation (golf) with Miss Blanchard and Reverend Mante in mind. I'm psyched whenever I prepare a sermon or stand at the first tee. And while I know

I can always recover from bad sermons and starts (shots), it saves time and tears when doing it right the first time.

Whether it's God or golf, *nothing can happen through you that has not first happened to you.* Or as one missionary said, "You can't give away what you ain't got for yourself!"

In other words, if you're not exhilarated — *psyched* — whenever you enter the pulpit or tee it up, don't bother! Nobody wants to listen to or play with people who *obviously* don't care about what they're doing. That's why some churches are empty and some folks have problems getting partners.

I think of Milton the lawyer who reviewed documents from bond issues. His handicap was higher than New Jersey taxes. He approached his job and golf with the enthusiasm of someone being interviewed by Mike Wallace. So nobody wanted to work or play with him.

After about five holes of his firm's annual golf outing, his team walked off the course disgusted by his *underwhelming* approach to life and sport. So Milton caught up with the group on the next tee and asked if he could join them. Knowing his reputation, they said, "Sorry, Milton, but we've already got three."

Paul Azinger was playing with Gary Player on slow greens. Player remarked how he loved playing on slow greens. Then Azinger played with Player on fast greens. Player remarked how he loved playing on fast greens. So Azinger asked which was his favorite. And Player told him that the only way to enjoy the game is to enjoy the whole game.

I remember John Huffman telling me about Norman Vincent Peale's evaluation of him early in ministry which John was reciting as a caution to me early in ministry. Dr. Peale told John that he was like fireworks — bright and brilliant and exciting and attractive and effective. But if he didn't pace himself for the long haul, Dr. Peale said his ministry would burn brightly but briefly with only ashes remaining to trace his ministry.

Whether it's the first hole or the first day on the job, it doesn't end at the beginning. Pacing for the long haul is the path to success. Or as Reverend Mante challenged me years ago: Be slow! Be steady! Be solid!

And yet the first hole and first day set the tone for what's ahead. My dad likes to say, "Start strong and stay strong and you'll succeed." Arnold Palmer put it this way (*My Game and Yours*, 1983):

> *Oh, it's great to overcome a bad start and come from behind, but it isn't easy. A bad start can discourage you, throwing your game off completely. We pros sometimes find that we have shot ourselves right out of a tournament on the first nine. The average player, if he starts off badly, finds it almost impossible to pull his game together. His confidence and concentration are gone for the day; he may as well go home ... How much better it is to start off as a firecracker and not have to come from behind ... For another, a good start sets you up mentally and gives you the confidence you need to keep playing your best.*

And then putting the paradox together — recovery is possible but a good start is preferable — the king went on:

> *You have to keep reminding yourself all the time that the first three holes count, for it's easy to forget. Even in an eighteen-hole round the whole day seems to loom ahead of you. If you lose the first hole, there's always the second. And if you lose the second hole, too, there are sixteen to go ... But if you fall into this lackadaisical mental trap, your day can be ruined before you know it ... the rest of the round is just a chore and a nuisance. Chalk up another golf round spoiled by carelessness in the early stages.*

That's why the early church outlined a very simple strategy for a slow, steady, and solid start (Acts 2:42-47):

> *They devoted themselves to the apostles' teaching and fellowship, to the breaking of bread and the prayers. Awe came upon everyone, because many wonders and signs were being done by the apostles. All who believed were together and had all things in common; they*

12

*would sell their possessions and goods and distribute
the proceeds to all, as any had need. Day by day, as they
spent much time together in the temple, they broke
bread at home and ate their food with glad and
generous hearts, praising God and having the goodwill
of all the people. And day by day the Lord added to their
number those who were being saved.*

I think of Art in Winston-Salem, North Carolina. He made an
appointment to see me and began, "Dr. Kopp, you always talk about
a personal relationship with Jesus as the way to happiness, whole-
ness, joy, and eternal security. Well, how can I get that relationship?" I replied, "You won't *get it* with a snap of your fingers. It's
a process: worship, pray, read the Bible, hang out with Christians,
and take Holy Communion."

He did.

He did!

And Art is happy, whole, joyful, and secure.

I'm not saying every day at work will be a hot fudge sundae or
that first drive will always find the fairway more than a two minute
walk from the tee. I'm just saying the first day and first hole aren't
nearly as daunting when you're psyched, slow, steady, and solid.

13

Take Some Lessons

All scripture is inspired by God and is useful....
— 2 Timothy 3:16

My handicap was heading to single digits and those absurd late forty*ish* daydreams about the senior tour were making denominational meetings more tolerable when disaster struck.

Playing with my dad in one of those little *friendly-while-you're-winning* matches, I was even through fifteen holes. I had been slow, steady, and solid throughout the round. So I strutted to the sixteenth tee, undoubtedly more personally impressed than impressive.

Looking back, I was probably coming off as badly as the starlet who blurted out during an interview, "Well, well, well, that's enough about me. *What do you think of me?*"

Time has taught me to be careful while riding high in the saddle. You're an easy target. God always seems to have a Mount Gilboa around the corner for the arrogant. When you think you've arrived, God's providence has a way of letting you know there's still a long way to go.

Anyway, I nailed it. My drive landed about fifty yards from the pin on a hole measuring 390 yards.

Roll the video!

Swaggering to my ball with increasing obnoxiousness, I promptly shanked it into the woods.

I finished six over on the last three holes!

Understanding golf etiquette, nobody said a word as I butchered the once promising round and related to Dick Schaap's quip: "Golf is a bloodless sport — if you don't count ulcers."

The problem — *disease* — wouldn't go away. It followed me from Wilkes-Barre's Irem Temple Country Club to Canonsburg's Lindenwood Golf Course to Claysville's Dogwood Hills.

I completely concur with Harvey Penick: "A shank shot is so ugly that I hate to write the word. Let's call it a lateral shot instead."

15

All I know is players don't yell *shank* when they hit one.

The harder I tried to fix the fault *on my own*, the worse it got. After almost two weeks of ruined rounds, I called my dad and asked for help. He asked what I thought I was doing wrong. "If I knew that, Dad," I replied sarcastically, "I wouldn't be asking you."

At that moment, my dad could have responded in kind like Sam Snead once told a student, "Lay off three weeks and then quit for good." Or as Phyllis Diller disclosed for struggling hackers, "The reason the pro tells you to keep your head down is so you can't see him laughing."

Instead, he repeated the question. My dad has always been patient with his son. He reminds me of another *Father* and His children.

After I theorized the error as hitting the ball off the club's toe, my dad explained how a shank occurs when hitting the ball off the hosel. In other words, my cure for the disease — hitting the ball closer and closer to the hosel — was producing the opposite effect. The more I pursued my theory, the farther I moved from the truth.

Sometimes the truth eludes us. That's when we need to go to a pro and take some lessons.

The same goes for women and men of faith. Sometimes we just don't get it *on our own*. We need to go to the pro and take some lessons on life.

Paul put it this way, "All scripture is God-breathed and is useful for teaching, rebuking, correcting and training in righteousness, so that the man of God may be thoroughly equipped for every good work" (see 2 Timothy 3:16-17 NIV).

Moreover, women and men of faith have always looked to Jesus as the perfect pattern for life because he is the enfleshed God. Or as Paul explained, "All the fullness of God was pleased to dwell in him" (see Colossians 1). Or as a Sunday school teacher once defined incarnation for me, "Jesus is God *with skin on*."

That's why so many Christians are wearing bracelets, necklaces, T-shirts, hats, ties, lapel pins, and all the rest with WWJD on them (*viz.*, "What would Jesus do?").

He's the pro.

And that's why the best lessons for life are taught by Him.

Hale Irwin, arguably one of the top two or three senior players of all time who wasn't too shabby on the junior tour either, observed, "There are days when you play well and there are days when you learn."

The goal of golf is simple: put the ball in the hole with as few swings as possible.

How to reach the goal is the tough part.

It's the same for everything else.

It's easy to establish goals.

Reaching them is the tough part.

I think of the fellow who found a magic lamp while walking on a beach. He rubbed it and a genie appeared. "Before you get any ideas," the genie noted, "I'm only granting one wish today. So make it good." "Well," the man said, "I've always wanted to go to Hawaii. But I don't like to sail or fly. So build a highway from California to Hawaii." "Forget it," the genie said, "that's three thousand miles away. And can you imagine all the environmental restrictions? Give me another wish." The man reflected a moment and then said, "Well, I've always wanted to understand women. Explain women to me." Quickly, the genie asked, "Do you want a two or four lane highway?"

A couple met at Myrtle Beach and fell in love. As they discussed the future of the relationship, the man admitted: "It's only fair to tell you that I'm a golf nut. I eat, sleep, and breathe golf." "Since we're being honest," the woman admitted, "it's only fair to tell you that I'm a hooker." "I see," the man reacted pensively. Gathering himself after a long silence, he said with a smile, "It's probably because your in-to-out swing is too severe or you need to adjust your grip a little."

Whether it's golf or just about anything else, most things don't come *naturally*. Even when we *can* learn things on our own, there's usually a lot of trial, error, and pain along the way. That's why it's best to have a manual and mentor. It's best to read the instructions and pay attention to the teacher.

Sure, there are exceptions to the rule — those especially gifted *few* who pick it up all by themselves. Trevino. Rodriquez. Mozart. Einstein. *But there are only a few!* I haven't met or even heard of too many self-taught — I prefer to say divinely gifted — of any stripe who can say with Lee Tevino: "I've never had a coach in my life. When I find one who can beat me, I'll listen."

Most of us need help. Or as Johnny Miller acknowledged, "No one becomes a champion without help."

So the prerequisite to improvement is *recognizing the need for improvement.* "If you're serious about improving your play," Greg Norman urged, "be brutally honest with yourself." Improvement requires the humility of Harvey Penick: "I never know so much that I can't learn more." Or as Jack Nicklaus, golf history's greatest competitor, insisted: "Don't be too proud to take lessons. I'm not."

Again, if you think you've arrived, you've got a really long way to go.

One of the most apocalyptic moments in my life occurred when I was a fifth grader in Nanticoke, Pennsylvania's Lincoln Street School. We were having lunch in our home room. I watched Mr. Moore, our science as well as home room teacher, take out his false teeth to gum graham crackers. Then I looked over at Donna who exchanged penny candy for kisses in the cloakroom. She was winking at me. I winked back. I always liked licorice. Melvin had another puddle under his desk. And Marilyn who was in her third year of fifth grade started rubbing my back. I didn't stop her. And I thought to myself, "Everybody in here is messed up." Then it hit me! "If everybody in here is messed up," I reasoned, "then I must be messed up too."

It was an apocalyptic moment.

Everybody — including me — was messed up.

Everybody — including me — remains messed up.

It's that original sin thing. We don't need any help to do things badly. It comes to us *naturally.* But we need help to do things the right way. We need instructions.

While none of us is as bad as some suggest, none of us is as good as our moms pretend.

Everybody has room for improvement.

It's a major theme of Christianity.

Everybody has problems.

18

That's the bad news.

Here's the good news.

God loves us any way.

To paraphrase a popular person from Pittsburgh, "God loves you just the way you are, *but loves you too much to leave you just the way you are.*"

And by God's grace, we have a manual (the Bible) and a mentor (Jesus) to teach us how to improve.

However, no one takes lessons until she or he *confesses* the need for them.

That's another major theme of Christianity.

Confession precedes redemption.

And between confession and redemption is repentance, or turning away from people and actions that don't work to people and actions that do work. Repentance is turning away from who and what are bad and turning to who and what are good.

I'm reminded of this story from Ken Blanchard (*Playing the Great Game of Golf*, 1992):

> *You can't just wait for good to come your way. You have to take action. It's like the man who, every night for six months, had prayed to the Lord to let him win the lottery — but nothing happened. He became impatient. The next night when he knelt to pray, he was angry. He said to the Lord, "I can't understand why I haven't won the lottery yet. I've prayed every night for six months for it. I am a good person. I love my wife, I am good to my kids, and faithful to You. Why haven't I won the lottery yet?" There was a crack of lightning in the sky and a voice shouted down: "Give me a hand. Buy a ticket!"*

Billy Graham put it this way: "Prayer never seems to work for me on the golf course. I think this has something to do with my being a terrible putter."

If you've got a problem, see a pro!

Take some lessons!

Equipped To Play

Just as the United States Golf Association says, "I really, really, really love golf." It's fun, good exercise *without* a cart, an unconquerable adventure, and cheaper than a shrink.

That's why one of us confessed: "My wife said it's her or golf. Boy, am I going to miss my wife."

I'm kidding.

But there are some things that are really starting to bother me. The prize money on the three big tours is increasingly obscene and already unconscionable. And it's getting really, really, really expensive. The costs of equipment and play are escalating quicker than the price of a back-up quarterback in the NFL.

However, I'm not too concerned about the costs. They'll come down as the game's popularity mimics the growth and decline graphs of tennis, racketball, jogging, and so on. Indeed, I feel a little sorry for course owners, pro shops, manufacturers, and retailers whose price-gouging makes divorce lawyers blush. *What goes around comes around* and it's coming around for the golf industry right now according to the latest stock reports.

But if I could ever find a putter allergic to three-putt greens, I'd pay almost as much as Nevillewood's pro shop charges. "You never stop searching for the perfect putter," Nick Price noted just before the 1998 PGA Championship, "but this one has worked really well."

Yeah, right!

They all work *for a while.*

Bob Dehls, my favorite clubmaker and an elder at Center, often says, "Every club has a 45-day guarantee. After 45 days, you're looking for a new one." He also likes to say, "The toughest yardage in golf is between the ears." Or as Craig Stadler lamented, "Why am I using a new putter? Because the old one didn't float too well."

21

"The constant undying hope for improvement," Bernard Darwin concluded, "makes golf so exquisitely worth playing."

The passion for improvement drives people to all corners of the earth *or at least another catalogue* for that "this-is-my-last" driver or putter or wedge or glove or racket or rod or cue or bow or computer or whatever.

Terry Schwarzbach, a golfing buddy who knows even more about buying those *last* clubs than I do, rationalizes, "Buying new equipment is half the fun."

That's true, except for me when my wife confronts me with the Discover Card bill.

Theoretically and *really*, it's the pursuit of something *better.*

And it's as deluding as Monty Python's search for the Holy Grail.

It's the same with everything else.

One of my favorite commercials has a teenager looking into her closet which is packed tightly with clothes. She turns around in panic and screams, "Mom, school starts next week and I've got nothing to wear!"

It's the Imelda Marcos syndrome and we've all got it.

How many clubs or rackets or tools or computers or shoes or suits or necklaces or rings or belts or briefcases or purses or dolls or toys or trains or video games or ... (*It's a long list!*) ... do we need?

One of the Rockefellers liked to say: "How much is enough? *Just a little bit more than I have!*"

We'll save *simplifying our lifestyles* for another book or when Tony Campolo comes back to town.

Actually, we always save that discussion for another time that never comes.

But whether it's golf or some other therapeutic distraction, we're always looking for better equipment.

And by God's grace *or the dark side* depending upon your perspective, there's always somebody hawking that cure-all for what keeps us from *nirvana*.

Harvey Penick described how it goes (*And If You Play Golf, You're My Friend*, 1993):

For most everyone, the driver is the most difficult club
in the bag ... When a player finds a driver he falls in love
with, he keeps it forever — or at least until he falls out
of love and divorces the club and sends it to live with
eight or ten other drivers in the closet or the trunk of the
car ...
    I remember how in about 1962 a manufacturer
came out with a new driver that had some kind of slot in
the head that supposedly increased distance. One of my
Texas boys ... told me he wanted to buy the new driver
... There was nothing wrong with Billy's old driver, and
he was good with it. Like all golfers, Billy was being
gullible to the lure of advertising.

Theodore Jorgensen, a retired physics professor at the University of Nebraska, greeted another debut of better golf equipment this way: "The average golfer can improve his game quicker by improving his swing, rather than by trying to find equipment that works better."

Or as the seriously seasoned will tell you, "You can buy the best equipment but it won't make any difference until you learn how to play the game."

My dad often says: "It's not the equipment. It's the player. All clubs work if you know what you're doing. It's just a matter of aesthetics — looking down and liking what you see."

But then I gave him a Biggest Big Bertha for Father's Day.

Now he agrees with those who insist technological advances are making the game easier.

That's what Michael Murphy's Adam understood in *Golf in the Kingdom*:

    "Golf recapitulates evolution," he said in a melodious
voice, "it is a microcosm of the world, a projection of
all our hopes and fears." I cannot remember all the
phrases, but his words were an ecstatic hymn to golf ...
He told about the technological changes in the game
and how they brought new powers and awareness into
play for those who pursued it with a passion. With its
improved clubs and balls and courses, golf reflected

man's ever-increasing complexity. It was becoming a
better vehicle for training the higher capacities. And so
it was becoming the yoga of the supermind, the ultimate
discipline for transcendence.

Huh?

Murphy's metaphysics are a little far out. But, essentially, the message is everything evolves. And while cynics concentrate on the negatives of societal evolution, most of us see things getting better and better and better.

Foot. Horse. Automobile. Airplane.

Rock. Pencil. Typewriter. Computer.

Home remedy. Generalist. Specialist. Washington Hospital.

Ice. Fan. Air conditioning.

While it may come as a shock to fundamentalists, God can even work through evolution to bless us.

Everybody wants to get better at what she or he does at work and recreation. And God makes that possible by the progressive evolution of equipment.

A fellow said to a friend, "I got some new golf clubs for my wife." His friend remarked, "That's great! I wish I could make a trade like that."

Again, *I'm just kidding.*

But it's a tough game and it makes sense to play with the best equipment.

History has taught there are always new and improved ways of doing things.

If you think that's hooey or somehow alien to our ethic, you need to take another long look at our Lord's parable of the wineskins (see Matthew 9:17).

Life is tough too.

You know that.

There's no need to catalogue the crises.

You know them.

And many of you have already experienced more than your share of them.

24

We can be thankful that our Lord has provided the equipment to live triumphantly amid the meanness, madness, and misery of life in the modern world.

So many psalms remind us that God is our sustaining source of strength, stability, and sanity. I especially like these lines from Psalm 144: "Blessed be the Lord, my rock ... and my fortress, my stronghold and my deliverer, my shield, in whom I take refuge ... Happy are the people whose God is the Lord."

Or as we say, "Jesus saves."

Paul was more specific. He listed the equipment provided by God as "the full armor of God" (see Ephesians 6:10-20):

1. *The Belt of Truth* — Jesus!
2. *The Breastplate of Righteousness* — A holy life in Jesus!
3. *Shoes of Peace* — Walking the talk of Jesus!
4. *The Shield of Faith* — Assurance of salvation through Jesus!
5. *The Helmet of Salvation* — Jesus!
6. *The Sword of the Spirit* — The Bible which tells the truth of Jesus!

Simply, *Jesus*!

But listen very carefully.

The equipment won't fit until we get to know the manufacturer.

Putting it directly, Jesus doesn't make any difference in our lives until he is at the center *or heart* of our lives.

I think of what Roberto De Vicenzo said to Seve Ballesteros just before he won the 1979 British Open: "You have the hands, now play with your heart."

The equipment only becomes effective *after* it is embraced by the heart, soul, mind, and body.

Only then are we equipped to play.

And only after we invite Jesus into our hearts as Lord and Savior are we equipped for this life and the next.

Nancy Meider comes to mind.

The temple of her soul — her physical body — is dying of cancer *but her spirit survives in calm and certain expectation of the next chapter of her never-ending story as a child of God because she has Jesus in her heart as Lord and Savior.*

Her faith in Jesus has so equipped her for eternal victory over an existential disease that she inspires confidence and peace and joy in all who visit her.

I've often thought of "Footprints" after visiting Nancy. It's familiar to most of us:

> One night a man had a dream. He dreamed he was walking along the beach with the Lord. Across the sky flashed scenes from his life. For each scene, he noticed two sets of footprints in the sand, one belonging to him, and the other belonging to the Lord.
>
> When the last scene of his life flashed before him, he looked back at the footprints in the sand. He noticed that many times along the path of his life there was only one set of footprints. He also noticed that it happened at the very lowest and saddest times in his life.
>
> This really bothered him and he questioned the Lord about it. "Lord, You said that once I decided to follow You, You'd walk with me all the way. But I have noticed that during the most troublesome times in my life, there is only one set of footprints. I don't understand why when I needed you most you would leave me."
>
> The Lord replied, "My precious, precious child, I love you and I would never leave you. During your times of trial and suffering, when you saw only one set of footprints, it was then that I carried you."

Chances are you've heard that many times.

But like the old gospel song goes, "For those who know it best seem hungering and thirsting to hear it like the rest."

It's refreshing to be reminded God is with us at all times.

My friend Thom Hickling just sent me an update which he calls "A Variation on Footprints":

> Now imagine you and the Lord Jesus walking down the road together. For much of the way, the Lord's footprints go along steadily and consistently, rarely varying the pace. But your prints are disorganized, a

stream of zigzags, starts, stops, turnarounds, circles, departures and returns. For much of the way, it seems to go like this.

But gradually, your footprints come more in line with the Lord's soon paralleling His consistently. You and Jesus are walking as true friends.

This seems perfect, but then an interesting thing happens. Your footprints that were etched in the sand next to the Master's are now walking precisely in His steps. Inside His larger footprints is the small "sand-print," safely enclosed. You and Jesus are becoming one. This goes on for many miles.

But you notice another change. The footprint inside the larger footprint seems to grow larger. Eventually, it disappears altogether. There is only one set of footprints. They have become one. Again, this goes on for a long time.

But then something awful happens. The second set of footprints is back. And this time, it seems even worse. Zigzags all over the place. They stop. They start. Deep gashes in the sand. A veritable mess of prints. You're amazed and shocked. But this is the end of your dream.

Now you speak: "Lord, I understand the first scene with the zigzags and fits and starts and so on. I was a new Christian, just learning. But you walked on through the storm and helped me learn to walk with you."

"That is correct."

"Yes, and when the smaller footprints were inside of Yours, I was actually learning to walk in Your steps. I followed You very closely."

"Very good. You understand everything so far."

"Then the smaller footprints grew and eventually filled in with Yours. I suppose that I was actually growing so much that I was becoming like You in every way."

"Precisely."

"But this is my question. Lord, was there a regression or something? The footprints went back to two, and this time it was worse than the first."

27

*The Lord smiles, then laughs. He says, "You didn't
know? That was when we danced!"*

Nancy's soul dances even as her body passes.
That's what happens when you're *equipped*.
But remember, nothing fits until our Lord is at the center *or
heart* of our lives.
By the way, everybody plays.
So it makes sense to employ the best equipment.
Jesus!

The Upside Of The Practice—
Performance Equation

You reap whatever you sow. — Galatians 6:7b

Even as cancer continues to ravage her body, Nancy Meider's personal relationship with Jesus as saving Lord enables a joy to radiate from her soul, through her eyes, and into the hearts of all who are blessed to know her.

We've talked about many things over the past several months. We've been silly on occasion, serious when necessary, and direct at all times.

That's how it becomes when time spent far exceeds time left. It's easy to distinguish the important from the incidental when each breath could be the last.

When I leave Nancy and encounter folks so majorly obsessed with such minor details, I want to scream, "Get a life *before it's too late!*" But I bite my tongue and keep it in because I've learned it's better to talk to God about some people than to talk to some people about God.

Having grown up in a church that outlawed Santa, fearing the funny fat man in the red suit would detract from the reason for the season — *a suspicion that I have never shared!* — I am always amused by Nancy's Santa collection. But I'm not the proverbial church lady or guy who feels God has given her or him some kind of right to poke a nose into somebody else's private idiosyncracies. So I never asked until I realized I better ask before it's too late. Nancy's simple explanation came with a soul-*full* smile: "Ever since I was a child, I've always liked Santa because he's so jolly. I think that's what God wants for us."

She's right.

Jesus said, "I have said these things to you so that my joy may be in you, and that your joy may be complete" (John 15:11).

29

I know I'll be presiding at a memorial service for Nancy much sooner than her family, friends, and I would wish. Certainly, we will see grieving tears as testimony to God's goodness expressed through her. Undoubtedly, we will witness to her resurrection and the promise of eternal reunion. And we'll beg our Lord's comforting consolations for those remaining.

We'll also ask why God took Nancy from us instead of recalling a few cranks, kooks, and cruel characters. God knows the passing of some would evoke the refrain, "Ding! Dong! The witch is dead!" So we'll complain more than a little bit about God's not consulting us first for more appropriate alternatives.

Of course, we would never begrudge Nancy the faithful's reward of that perfect place of personal peace where "there will be no more death or mourning or crying or pain" (see Revelation 21). For as David A. Redding reasoned, "Anyone who feels sorry for a dead Christian, as though the poor chap were missing something, is himself missing the transfiguring promotion involved" (*Getting Through The Night*, 1972).

But we'll still wonder why someone as good and positive and jolly as Nancy had to go home now.

I think of a familiar story.

While contemplating eternity, two buddies entertain the possibility of golf courses in heaven. One dies, returns to his friend, and says: "I've got some good news and some bad news. The good news is there are golf courses in heaven. The bad news is you tee off tomorrow morning."

Faithful folks like Nancy don't believe in bad news. While this life is good with all of its affections and most of us aren't in a hurry to exit, the life to come is even better. It's *heavenly*. That's the ultimate assurance of Christianity.

But before our time comes *and it will come sooner or later* with Nancy welcoming us *or Nancy being welcomed by us*, it's not too early to take inventories of our lives.

How will we be remembered?

We will be remembered.

It has been suggested we live good and positive and jolly lives so the presiding pastors don't have to lie at our funerals.

It's the best use of the time that's left for us.

And our time on earth is not endless. Or as Nancy likes to say, "Make the most of life while it *lasts.* "

She knows.

She hopes we get the message.

The message — *let's say alarm clock!* — is ringing loud and clear for me these days.

My AARP card just came in the mail.

My sons joke about my hairline and waistline.

A friend who was strolling down the fairway with me asked if I had considered something called Grecian Formula 44.

I went to a school function and the mother of one of my son's classmates nauseatingly exclaimed, "Oh, Daniel, how good it is to see you bringing your grandpap!"

I guess people will think my youngest son Matthew has brought somebody from *the home* when I show up with him at school.

I'm thinking about using a cart.

And I just found myself saying to a seminarian who was lamenting the lack of time to get things done: "You've got 42 years to go. I'm eligible for retirement in sixteen years."

I was not comforted.

But I have been challenged as well as reminded by all of the above that I don't have forever to reach my goals.

It's been said, "Someday everybody will return from the cemetery *but you.*"

Well, I'm determined to beat the hearse to my goals — not frenetically but slowly, steadily, and solidly.

Whenever I'm tempted to postpone my quest, I recall this story from *Tales of a Magic Monastery* (1981):

> *I had just one desire — to give myself completely to God. So I headed for the monastery. An old monk asked me, "What is it you want?"*
>
> *I said, "I just want to give myself to God."*
>
> *I expected him to be gentle, fatherly, but he shouted at me, "NOW!" I was stunned. He shouted again, "NOW!" Then he reached for a club and came after*

me. I turned and ran. He kept coming after me, brand-
ishing his club and shouting, "Now, Now."
That was years ago. He still follows me, wherever
I go. Always that stick, always that "NOW!"

What are you waiting for?

Will you still be waiting when it's too late?

Now!

You may have heard about the man who always complained about the peanut butter and jelly sandwiches in his lunch box. A friend asked, "Why don't you just ask your wife to make a different kind of sandwich every now and then?" The man replied, "I make my own lunches."

We make our own lunches.

The point is we *can't* reach our goals without *working* to reach them.

Ben Hogan often said, "Every day you miss playing or practicing is one day longer it takes to be good."

Every day we're not praying and working to reach our goals is one day longer it will take to reach them.

Every day we're not praying and working to be *His* in all things at all times is one day longer it will take to be *His* in all things at all times.

What are you waiting for?

Will you still be waiting when it's too late?

All of the above reminds me that we don't have forever to reach our goals.

That's why champions in every walk of life work so hard *every* day!

You may have seen Lee Trevino's commercial for Top Flite golf balls. He holds up a ball and says, "This ball will improve your game." Then he adds, "Of course, it will really help if you hit it 500 times a day."

By the time my son Ben was a senior in high school, it was obvious that our Lord had given him the gifts for athletic success. So I wrote this to him:

How To Become A Champion

Our Lord gives you the raw material:
smarts, speed, size, and the support of family,
friends, coaches, and school!

Only *you* develop the raw material
into a finished product.

If *you* fully develop what our Lord has given you;
you are a champion!

If *you* become God's best for your life,
you are a champion!

A champion does not do what is expected.
A champion does more than what is expected.

A champion runs the extra mile, lifts the extra weight,
and asks how she or he can develop God's best for
her or his life.

BE A CHAMPION!

You will be glad you did.
And the world will be better for it.

My dad likes to say, "The harder you work, the luckier you get."
The truth is work lessens the need for luck.

Or as Jack Nicklaus advised, "Learn the fundamentals of the
game and stick to them. Band-Aid remedies never last."

Paul put it this way, "You reap whatever you sow" (Galatians
6:7b).

I think of it as the practice-performance equation. Simply, practice equals performance. Specifically,

Bad Practice = Bad Performance
Mediocre Practice = Mediocre Performance
Good Practice = Good Performance

33

Better Practice = Better Performance
Excellent Practice = Excellent Performance

The upside of the practice-performance equation is we get out of life what we put into it.

It's true for golf, football, bowling, tennis, art, academics, music, and everything else including faith.

Or as Tim Johns told me may years ago: "The holier we are, the happier we are. If we want to be happier, we must become holier."

Ben Hogan concluded, "The ultimate judge of your swing is the flight of the ball."

Just as the quality of our practice is measured in golf by the performance recorded on the scorecard, the quality of the practice of our faith is measured by how we react to the ups and especially the downs of life.

Again, Nancy Meider knows all about that. She knows all about the downs of life.

But she also knows how to triumph over them.

She *rises above them* with Jesus.

It's the attitudinal difference between those who walk the talk and those who just talk. Those who just talk say, "It's raining. I think I'll exercise tomorrow." Those who walk the talk say, "It's raining. I'll put on rain gear so I don't miss a day of exercise."

Jesus explained (see Matthew 7:24 - 27):

Everyone then who hears these words of mine and acts on them will be like a wise man who built his house on rock. The rain fell, the floods came, and the winds blew and beat on that house, but it did not fall, because it had been founded on rock. And everyone who hears these words of mine and does not act of them will be like a foolish man who built his house on sand. The rain fell, and the floods came, and the winds blew and beat against that house, and it fell — and great was its fall!

Before he died, Tony Lema said: "I cling to a few tattered old virtues, like believing you don't get anything in this world for

34

nothing. This is one of those eternal verities that will be around long after I've sunk my last putt and gone to that great nineteenth hole in the sky."

It's the practice-performance equation.

And when it comes to the movement from our existential to eternal relationship with God, we could say practice makes perfect.

The Downside Of The Practice – Performance Equation

We know that all things work together for good for
those who love God.... — Romans 8:28

I'm glad I'm a man.

As my son was being born 22 years ago, two thoughts came to mind. First, "What a miracle!" Second, "Thank You, Jesus, for making me a man because I could never do that!" It's like Joan Rivers said, "If a man wants to know what it's like to give birth, all he has to do is take his upper lip and pull it over his head."

I'm also aware of sexism in society and church.

But as a beneficiary of sexism because of my gender, I've often shrugged it off.

Back in my second year of seminary, a whole bunch of women were admitted to Princeton. A high-ranking administrator confided to me, "Women who take the place of men in seminaries will cause the opposite effect of what was intended. Instead of opening new pulpits for women, it will allow men to be more selective. It will also open pulpits to our worst male graduates." There was locker room talk about female seminarians being less interested in an M.Div. than an Mrs. *I shrugged it off.*

Though I've been an integral part of calling seven or eight associate pastors, only one was a woman. The Reverend Ilona J. Buzick was called as associate pastor of Kansas City's Second Presbyterian Church in the early 1980s. She was the first female pastor on staff. There was one elder who said he'd never worship when she preached because of her gender. *I shrugged it off.*

I've always thought of myself as gender inclusive. I've always tried to ensure gender balance on church committees. But when it hasn't happened, *I've shrugged it off.*

I've always voted for the best person regardless of gender. But when a woman of greater qualifications has lost to a man of lesser qualifications, *I've shrugged it off.*

While I currently head a staff dominated by women and appreciate the lack of evidence to accuse me of gender bias, I know that guys in similar positions always receive greater compensatory considerations. *I shrugged it off in the past. Now I can't get away with it.*

But sexism really hit home when my sister became a victim.

Sue entered a golf tournament sponsored by the Friendly Sons of Saint Patrick at a modest course called Four Seasons just outside of Wilkes-Barre, Pennsylvania. FSSP is a benevolent fraternity — meaning they do some good things while hanging out with the boys and boozing it up.

Being one of the area's better female golfers, it wasn't surprising that Sue won gender competitions for closest to the pin and longest drive. What was surprising — *disgusting* — was the disparity of awards based on gender. While men received equipment and apparel, my sister got a lasagna pan and a cheap umbrella.

I'm embarrassed to say I shrugged off sexism until it hit home. I'm sorry it took the victimization of a relative to open my eyes and *spirit* to this sin.

I should have gotten the message years ago from our Lord: "In everything do to others as you would have them do to you; for this is the law and the prophets" (Matthew 7:12).

I'm still glad I'm a man because of the birth thing.

I'll be a much better one when I start acting with gender fairness off and on the course. I'll be a *friendly son of God* when I stop shrugging off sexism and start standing up for equal opportunity as well as responsibility.

Sometimes we do our best and still fall flat, fail, or get the short end of the stick.

I think of the wife who adored her husband. "If I die," she teased during a candlelight dinner on their anniversary, "will you marry again?" "Probably," came the dispassionate reply. "Well," she went on, "will you give her my clothes and jewelry?" "Probably," came the dispassionate reply again. Increasingly irritated, she asked, "How about the house and car? Will you give them to her too?" "Probably," came the dispassionate reply once more.

Sarcastically, she asked, "How about my golf clubs?" "No," he answered, "she's left-handed."

I don't know if that story inspired him, but Dr. Addison Leitch, the great theologian and seminary president from Pittsburgh, often said, "Life keeps coming at you left-handed."

It's called *the rub of the green* in golf. You hit a great shot and it takes a bad bounce into a hazard. Arnold Palmer has said many times, "Golf is full of perfect shots that end in disaster." Marino Parascenzo theorized, "In football some coaches have stated, 'When you throw a pass, three things can happen, two of them are bad.' In golf, there is no limit." Or as Sam Snead told Ted Williams after one of the greatest hitters of baseball history insisted baseball is much harder to play than golf because a batter has to hit a ball traveling so fast, "Yeah, Ted, but you don't have to go up in the stands and play your foul balls."

While the rub of the green can end up in your favor — a bad shot taking a good bounce — most golfers get rubbed the wrong way regularly.

No one is immune to life's bad bounces. You do your best as a wife or husband and the marriage still turns sour. You do your best as parents and the kids still get into trouble. You do your best at work and still get laid off or fired or remain under-compensated.

Sometimes the practice-performance equation doesn't work. Sometimes the best practice yields the worst performance.

Or as Bruce Lansky lamented: "My golf pro said, 'Practice makes perfect.' He lied."

While the practice-performance equation *usually* works, sometimes it doesn't. Sometimes we do our best and still fall flat, fail, or get the short end of the stick. Sometimes we do our best and fall short of our goals. That's the downside of the practice-performance equation.

One of the most spectacular stories in golf history occurred on the eighteenth hole at St. Andrews during the final round of the 1995 British Open. Constantino Rocca of Italy needed to get down in two to tie American John Daly and force a playoff. Only a chip and putt from his goal, he totally blew the chip. But instead of giving up, he composed himself and gallantly sunk a seemingly impossible thirty-footer to send the British Open into a playoff.

Then John Daly completely crushed him in the playoff to win his second major championship. Rocca did his best and still fell short of the prize. It happens all the time.

That's why I tell new pastors: "If you want people to bleed for Jesus, you'll have to hemorrhage. But just because you're bleeding to death doesn't mean anybody is going to show up to give blood."

Parenthetically — and please indulge these comments as a warning to your children — I don't know anyone in her or his right mind who would *want* to become a pastor. You never get to spend the holidays with your family. You get paid less than you know you deserve and more than most people pretend you deserve. You're humiliated at least once a year at an annual meeting when you have to get out of the room so people have a chance to gutlessly talk behind your back and vote on your salary. You don't get to talk back to people who mouth off to you. And everybody thinks she or he can tell you what to do when you've been called to pay attention to only *One*.

I feel much better now.

New or prospective pastors probably feel worse.

So let me do an old Raider Ben Davidson thing and pile on.

If you would like to know what it's like to be a pastor, put on a deerskin and go walking through the woods on the first day of hunting season.

I don't know why anyone in her or his right mind would *want* to become a pastor unless, of course, you know, they're called to do it.

The same goes for everybody and everything else. You do what you're called to do without regard to the bad bounces.

Ultimately, success is not measured by the scorecard or payoff or salary or trophy or plaque or diploma or gold watch or whatever. Success is faithfulness to God's will for our lives without regard to the existential results.

Paul knew we'd experience bad bounces. He said, "All have sinned and fall short of the glory of God" (Romans 3:23). Some bad bounces will result from bad shots. Sometimes we'll be victims of life's bad bounces. But one way or the other, no one is immune to life's bad bounces. And the only way to rise above them is to remain faithful to God's will for our lives. Or as Habakkuk explained (2:4; 3:17-19):

> *The righteous live by their faith.*
>
> *Though the fig tree does not blossom, and no fruit is on the vines; though the produce of the olive fails and the fields yield no food; though the flock is cut off from the fold and there is no herd in the stalls, yet I will rejoice in the Lord; I will exult in the God of my salvation.*
>
> *God, the Lord, is my strength; he makes my feet like the feet of a deer, and makes me tread upon the heights.*

I think that's the meaning of God's promise through Paul: "We know that all things work together for good for those who love God" (Romans 8:28).

I've always thought Paul left out the word *eventually.*

Anyway, I think of a story sent to me by Melissa Hinnebusch:

> *Many years ago, the President of Harvard made a mistake by prejudging people and it cost him dearly.*
>
> *A woman in a faded gingham dress and her husband dressed in a homespun threadbare suit stepped off the train in Boston and walked timidly without an appointment into the president's outer office.*
>
> *The secretary could tell in a moment that such backwards country hicks had no business at Harvard and probably didn't even deserve to be in Cambridge. She frowned. "We want to see the president," the man said softly. "He'll be busy all day," the secretary snapped. "We'll wait," the woman replied.*
>
> *The secretary ignored them for hours, hoping they would become discouraged and go away.*
>
> *They didn't.*

The secretary grew frustrated and finally decided to disturb the president, even though she didn't want to do it. "Maybe if they just see you for a few minutes, they'll leave," she told him. He nodded agreement in exasperation.

Someone of his importance obviously didn't have the time to spend with them. Moreover, he detested gingham dresses and homespun suits cluttering up his outer office. Stern-faced with practiced dignity, the president strutted toward the couple.

The woman said, "We had a son who attended Harvard for one year. He loved Harvard. He was happy here. But about a year ago, he was killed accidentally. So my husband and I would like to erect a memorial to him somewhere on campus."

Instead of being touched, the president was incensed. "Madam," he said gruffly, "we can't put up a statue for every person who attended Harvard and died. If we did, this place would look like a cemetery."

"Oh, no," the woman explained quickly, "we don't want to erect a statue. We thought we would like to give a building to Harvard."

The president rolled his eyes. He glanced at the gingham dress and homespun suit and then exclaimed, "A building! Do you have any earthly idea how much a building costs? We have over seven and a half million dollars in the physical plant at Harvard."

The woman was silent.

The president was pleased. He thought he could get rid of them now.

Then the woman turned to her husband and said, "Is that all it costs to start a university? Why don't we just start our own?"

Her husband nodded.

Mr. and Mrs. Leland Stanford walked away, traveled to Palo Alto, California, and built a university which bears their name as a memorial to a son that Harvard didn't care about.

I also think of Jodie Harrison. Jodie was dying of cancer. I prayed healing for Jodie. Following the prescription of James 5:13-16, I anointed her with oil and laid hands on her with other elders. We shared the sacrament regularly. And on the day before she died, I said: "Jodie, I'm really sorry. I thought for sure that God had healed you. I'm really sorry."

She said: "Bob, we prayed for healing and God gave me the greatest healing of all. My family was fractured. They never got together and never had a kind word to say about each other. But my passing has brought them together. I prayed God would heal my family for many years. He used my death to heal my family. I'm so thankful. Besides, I'm going to heaven. That's not so bad."

When we're faced with life's bad bounces, it helps to look at the cross. The cross was the precursor to total victory.

Every cross in a Christian's life is a precursor to total victory.

Again, "We know that all things work together for good for those who love God."

Or as a little card on my desk says, "When you think you haven't got a prayer, He's there!"

I guess there really isn't a downside to faith.

Golfers say, "A bad day of golf is better than any day without golf."

Robert Schuller says, "God turns our scars into stars!"

I like that. I like *Him*.

I'm glad God doesn't shrug us off.

No matter how the ball bounces or how bad a day has been, the final score is already in the book.

We're saved.

Take Dead Aim

Let us fix our eyes on Jesus. —Hebrews 12:2 (NIV)

My wife and I were discussing the state of *affairs* in America. I said every child of the 1960s knew there was a credibility gap when he said he didn't inhale.

I said every golfer knew character would be a continuing issue after correspondents for several golf magazines caught him cheating during a round with two of his predecessors.

I said everybody knows he cheated on his wife for years and lied to family, friends, colleagues, and employees.

I said he admitted to an inappropriate — s-e-x-u-a-l — relationship with an intern just a little bit older than his daughter.

My wife said she thought she knew who I was talking about but my description fits a large percentage of America's male population.

Touché!

Maybe that's why he remains so popular.

He's just like us.

When America looks in the mirror, it sees him.

My wife also said it's hard to throw stones when you live in a glass house.

I think she was saying that if we went after him, it wouldn't be long before they come after us.

As she spoke, I thought I heard a voice, "What's that I see in your eye?"

Whenever we try to make our heroes into something a little more than human, we get into trouble. They're just not up to it.

Just look at the rap sheets of our heroes. Adam and Eve had bad diets. Moses was a murderer. Samson fell for Delilah. *See!* David just had to have Bathsheba. *See again!* Thomas Jefferson could really write about life and liberty while enslaving people. Babe Ruth struck out a lot and not just on the diamond. Mickey Mantle was a drunk. Mike Tyson bit off more than he could chew.

Cross-waving Evander Holyfield has six children by six different women. Tiger Woods can't win every week. We could go on and on and on.

It's just like Ralph Waldo Emerson said, "Every hero becomes at last a bore."

I prefer to say every hero becomes at last just *human*.

I'm not making excuses for you know who.

God forbid any of us embrace the kind of ethical amnesia that prompted Kentucky Senator Augustus Owsley Stanley to say back in the 1920s: "If Governor Fields is right, I am going to stand by him because he is right. If he is wrong, I am going to stand by him because he is a Democrat."

God forbid any of us mimic those mindless drones known as straight-ticket Democrats and Republicans who would vote for Satan if he were their party's nominee.

I'm just asking us to remember our faith includes the opportunity for redemption after confession and repentance.

Unfortunately, we've got this beastial habit in America of building up our human heroes and then tearing them apart because they're human.

Fortunately, God is a lot more gracious. I like the way the incarnate God Jesus put it, "God did not send the Son into the world to condemn the world, but in order that the world might be saved through him."

So if you're looking for a hero, I'd turn to God as expressed in Jesus. He's *divine* enough to deal with our humanity. He is the friend on whom we can rely in all things.

Ralph Earle, the great biblical scholar who taught at Kansas City's Nazarene Theological Seminary and helped edit *The New International Version* of the Bible, often told the story of John G. Paton who was a pioneer missionary to the New Hebrides. Dr. Paton soon discovered that while the natives had words for house, tree, stone, and the like, they had no words for love, joy, and peace. Worst of all, they had no word for believe. One day as he sat in his hut filled with frustration, an old native entered and slumped down in a chair. Exhausted from a long journey, the man said, "I'm leaning my whole weight on this chair." "What did you say?" asked

46

Dr. Paton. The man repeated, "I'm leaning my whole weight on this chair." Immediately, Dr. Paton cried, "That's it!" And from that day forward for that primitive tribe, "Believe in Jesus" became "Lean your whole weight on Jesus."

When Larry King asked Chuck Colson how he managed to avoid the troubles of so many church leaders, he said: "I tell people, 'Don't follow me! Follow Jesus!' "

Whether it's a parent, professor, pastor, president, or anybody else, human heroes always end up a little too *human*. They always end up disappointing our *larger than life* expectations. Aside from breaking the commandment about having only one God (see Exodus 20:3), *human* heroes just aren't up to *divine* prerogatives.

That's why Paul so mockingly addressed the people in the middle of the Areopagus (see Acts 17:16ff NIV): "Men of Athens, I see that in every way you are very religious. For as I walked around and looked carefully at your objects of worship, I found an altar with this inscription, 'To an unknown god.' "

Or as the Psalmist simply prescribed, "It is better to take refuge in the Lord than to trust in man. It is better to take refuge in the Lord than to trust in princes" (see Psalm 118 NIV).

Today, we might say, "It is better to take refuge in the Lord than to trust in professors, pastors, presidents, or anyone else who is less than divine."

Get it?

Only Jesus is divine. He alone is worthy of absolute trust.

As Hebrews 12:2 urges, "Let us fix our eyes on Jesus!" We need to aim higher than humanity for our heroes.

Golfers know the importance of focus — decisively picking a target and *going for it*.

Harvey Penick was famous for saying, "Take dead aim!" He wrote:

> *Instead of worrying about making a fool of yourself in front of a crowd of 4 or 40,000, forget about how your swing may look and concentrate instead on where you want the ball to go. Pretty is as pretty does ...*

47

Take dead aim at a spot on the fairway or the green, refuse to allow any negative thought to enter your head, and swing away.

A high handicapper will be surprised at how often the mind will make the muscles hit the ball to the target, even with a far less than perfect swing ...

Indecision is a killer ...

That's what I mean by taking dead aim. I mean clearing the mind of all thoughts except the thoughts of the target, so that the muscles are free to do the job.

Christians take dead aim at Jesus.

Christians focus on Jesus as the perfect pattern for faith and life.

Christians approach every decision of life with two questions: What would Jesus say about it? What would Jesus do about it?

Or as Jerry Kirk described the mission of the church for me many years ago, "We are called to be and do everything God calls us to be and do as exemplified in Jesus and explained in the Bible."

The golfer's goal is simple: "Keep on hitting it straight until the wee ball goes into the hole" (James Braid).

The Christian's goal is simple: "Be like Jesus!"

That's what *Christian* means — a representation of Jesus or a *little Christ.*

Christians want to grow up to be just like Jesus.

In other words, Christians have a better model than any professor, pastor, president, and so on.

Dr. Bob Rotella, Director of Sports Psychology at the University of Virginia and consultant to many of golf's greatest players, explained the efficacy of goal-setting (*Golf Is Not a Game of Perfect*, 1995):

A person with great dreams can achieve great things.

A person with small dreams, or a person without the confidence to pursue his or her dreams, has consigned himself or herself to a life of frustration and mediocrity.

The sage of Proverbs put it this way, "Where there is no vision, the people perish" (Proverbs 29:18, paraphrase).

Before the Reverend Ilona J. Buzick would accept a call to be associate pastor of Kansas City, Missouri's Second Presbyterian Church, she asked me: "Does the church want to grow? Does the church want to get better? Does it want to do great things for the Lord? Because if it doesn't, then I'm not called to it. I believe God has called me to be in life and ministry with people who want to be obedient to God's call to get better."

Unless God is dead, churches and their people can get better. They can grow. They can do more for God in mission, evangelism, educational opportunities, and all the rest. There's always room for growth unless, of course, God or we are dead.

I think of these lines which I came across not too long ago: "Everything that can be invented already has been." This statement was released in 1899 by the U.S. Patent Office. If these "experts" ran the world we would still be sitting in the dark. It is our responsibility to shatter outdated thinking and explore the realm of the untested; it is here that breakthrough opportunities are waiting to be discovered.

Can you imagine what our country or church would look like today if our predecessors said, "Well, that's enough! No need to get better!"?

Can you imagine what our country or church *will* look like if we say, "Well, that's enough! No need to get better!"?

Here are a few more challenging lines:

> *This is the beginning of a new day. You have been given this day to use as you will. You can waste it or use it for good. What you do today is important because you are exchanging a day of your life for it. When tomorrow comes, this day will be gone forever; in its place is something that you have left behind ... let it be something good.*

What have we invented?
What have we done?
What are we leaving behind?

Do we have high standards?
Do we have goals?
Are we taking dead aim at Jesus?
There's an easy way to find out.

I think of the woman who had an appendectomy. She asked her doctor, "Will the scar show when I'm at the beach?" The doctor answered, "That depends on you."

Martin Luther said, "Good works don't make a person good *but a good person does good works.*"

John Calvin said we show "the signs of our salvation."

Jesus said, "Follow me!"

Take dead aim!

Focus!

Be faithful!

Be The Ball

... I no longer live, but Christ lives in me.
— Galatians 2:20 (NIV)

I guess I'll never be *Mormon of the Year.*

Let me explain.

I wrote an article not too long ago about prayer in public schools. Before suggesting putting prayer back into public schools might be the cure for what ails us, I noted Christians don't want their children led in prayer by non-Christians as much as non-Christians don't want their children led in prayer by Christians.

Trying to be a little lyrical with a touch of *serious* humor, I reasoned, "*As a Christian,* I believe Jesus is who he said he is. That has made me very nervous about who might lead the prayers in public schools. *As a Christian,* I don't want my children led in prayer by Mormons, Muslims, Moonies, or anyone else with a less than divine estimate of Jesus."

Aside from provoking one especially politically correct*ed* clergyman to accuse me of everything from intentionally walking Sammy Sosa to participating in the Holocaust, it wasn't a big hit with two Mormons who really blasted me.

One dropped off a testy note at the church to tell me that I don't know what I'm talking about while the other wrote a letter to the editor to tell everybody that I don't know what I'm talking about.

Essentially, they wanted me to acknowledge Mormons as Christians.

Okay. Mormons are Christians. That's cool for politically correct public consumption. *But that's not correct considering New Testament Christology.*

There are significant differences between Mormons and *other* Christians. The truth is all of the traditional Protestant denominations, Roman Catholics, Nazarenes, Pentecostals, and so on do not recognize Mormonism as consistent with New Testament

Christology. And before you shoot the messenger, go to your local *Christian* bookstore and check out which section includes books about Mormons.

Calling their religion the Church of *Jesus Christ* of Latter Day Saints makes Mormons into New Testament Christians about as much as walking into McDonald's makes me into a Big Mac or playing with Pings makes me into Billy Mayfair. Just to set the record straight, claiming to be a New Testament Christian isn't enough. Last time I checked, that was the claim of Applewhite, Berg, Jones, Koresh, Hitler, and the like.

Simply and most significantly, New Testament Christians believe Jesus is uniquely Lord and Savior — one of the three ways the one God has made Himself known to us (*viz.*, Father, Son, and Holy Spirit). New Testament Christians believe in one God manifested in three ways — *una substantia et tres personae.*

Conversely, Mormons believe in Father, Son, and Holy Spirit as each being a god. Okay. If Mormons want to consider that Christianity, that's cool. *But that's not consistent with New Testament Christology and just about everybody else in Christendom.*

Again, there are many other differences but contradicting Christologies is the biggest.

Having said all of that, I like Mormons. I think they're great. Though their clean-cut-Mister-Clean missionaries always show up when I'm trying to watch a Pitt football game, I've always found Mormons to be cordial and cooperative as well as solid citizens. God knows the rest of us could learn a lot from them about devotion to family and faith. Indeed, there's a story floating around our corner of the Kingdom that says the difference between Mormons and Presbyterians is Mormons have something to say after they knock on the door. Moreover, some of my favorite golfers are Mormons.

That's my way of saying I like Mormons *personally* but disagree with them *prophetically* and doubt either of us makes good targets for *proselytizing.*

It's a big country with room for 57 varieties of religious expressions *as long as we're honest about our differences as a prelude to working on the universal ethic of unconditional love.*

I think of a conversation between Christian clergy and rabbis in Cranford, New Jersey, many years ago to discuss manger scenes on public properties. After I addressed the assembly and outlined the irreconcilable theological difference — Jesus — an old rabbi stood and said: "My young Christian friend is right. And I'll be damned if he's right. But I'm betting my soul that he is wrong just as he is betting his soul that he is right."

Let me get to the point.

Salvation belongs to God alone. I'm a little too *human* to be the judge of that.

But I do know the honesty of that meeting in New Jersey enhanced interfaith dialogue and service. Admitting our differences established mutual trust and enabled the pursuit of common goals.

Now before you call or write to confront me about how right you are and how wrong I am, let me share two lines from some nuns in Maryland: "If you're wrong, you can't afford to argue. If you're right, you don't need to."

Besides, it will all clear up in the end.

While studying in Heidelberg, Germany, in 1973, one of my professors was Dr. Wolfgang Löwe. Dr. Löwe was an engaging though eccentric theologian who called himself, in private, a Christian-Marxist.

Like most American students studying abroad and preparing for graduate schools, I was a real brown-noser. Having been a professor since those days, I confess liking students who brown-nosed me. It's so different from the church. Students are after grades and recommendations. So they tell you how great you are. They may not mean it, but they behave as if they do. It's a lot different from being the pastor of a church.

Anyway, my brown-nosing technique with Dr. Löwe was to tell him how much I knew about Karl Marx and quote him extensively in class and on paper.

Dr. Löwe called me into his office for what I thought would be the payoff. Instead, he said, "Herr Kopp, I know you are an American theological student preparing to enter Princeton. I know you intend to be a Christian pastor or professor. Please start talking like a Christian and stop talking like a Marxist so I can trust you."

In other words, be *authentic.*

Be *real.*

Be *yourself.*

Unfortunately, too many of us bring to mind the *Hagar the Horrible* cartoon in which a monk says, "I think therefore I am." Hagar's dimwitted friend blurts out, "So where does that leave me?"

As we've learned from that Heritage place in North Carolina starring Jim and Tammy Faye, Swaggert's teary-eyed confession from Louisiana, and the pathetic soundings from Pennsylvania Avenue, honesty is the best policy.

Honesty begins with a credible estimate of self.

After establishing who we are, only then can we work and pray for who we ought to be.

When I played competitive tennis, I discovered my winning percentage was directly related *to feeling the tennis racket was an extension or even a part of my arm.* If I could feel the ball on the strings of the racket as if I were holding the ball in my hand, I knew there would be trouble on the other side of the net.

After I injured my foot in the semifinal of a doubles tournament in Toledo, Ohio, I turned to golf and discovered the same principle held true. When I feel the ball coming off the club as if I were throwing it with my hand, I know I'm going to score well.

That's why mystical golfers say, "*Be* the ball!"

Michael Murphy's gurus in *Golf in the Kingdom* (1972) illustrate the point:

> *I had overheard Shivas telling his pupil to think of the ball and "sweet spot" belonging together ... Shivas had told MacIver that the ball and sweet spot were "already joined." "Just see it that way," he had said, "they're aye joined afore ye started playin'." The advice helped. I began to imagine them fitting together as I laid the club head behind the ball. It helped settle me down ... I continued thinking that the club face and the ball were one.*

Be the ball.

54

If you've ever played golf with someone like Jack Osburn, you know what I'm talking about. Jack really knows how to *address* the ball: "C'mon, ball! I've been good to you all day. I haven't lost you. C'mon, ball! Get in the hole!"

Some folks refer to it as visualization or seeing the result as integral to realizing the result.

Jerry Heard explained the benefits of visualization or *being the ball* in *The Golf Secrets of the Big-Money Pros* (1992):

> *Visualization is what we do before we stand up to hit each and every golf shot ... We stand directly behind the ball and the target ... We imagine the impact of the club hitting the ball ... We see the gentle arc of the ball in the air ... We witness the ball hitting the surface of the green ... We watch as it bounces and rolls toward the pin ... We see it follow the contours of the green as it approaches the cup ... And we see it deftly strike the pin and vanish into the hole.*

He went on:

> *And remember this important key — the more vividly detailed you picture this happening in your mind, the more successful you will be.*
>
> *Now all this may sound like pretty weird stuff, but when you think about it, it makes a lot of sense. What I've mentioned before about "focusing out" is really a form of clearing your mind of all negative thinking ... When you take the time to "visualize" a successfully executed shot in a very detailed way, you are actually replacing those negative thoughts with a solid positive thought ... pushing those negative thoughts out of the way. Believe me, it works!*

Just ask Mark McGwire and Sammy Sosa. They visualized their way to Ruthian records in the baseball season of 1998. Do you remember watching them as they visualized homers in the on deck circle?

It works!

"It is the art of putting onto your internal movie screen," reported Peter Ballingall in *Golf Practice Drills* (1995), "an image that depicts success."

Do you remember those marvelous scenes in *Amadeus* as Mozart walked through the village visualizing great musical masterpieces?

It works!

More often than not, we are who we think we are and achieve what we aspire to achieve. Bad thoughts equal bad results.

"I never really dreamed of making many putts," confessed Calvin Peete. "Maybe that's why I haven't made many."

Good thoughts equal good results. "We create success or failure on the course," Gary Player indicated and *incarnated*, "primarily by our thoughts."

Be the ball. The same goes for tennis, bowling, baseball, football, soccer, music, art, and everything else.

And the same goes for Christianity. If we want to be Christians, we've got to be *like* Jesus.

Be a *Christian* — a representation of Jesus in the world — a little Christ.

Or as Paul explained the goal of discipleship, "I no longer live, but Christ lives in me" (Galatians 2:20 NIV).

If Jesus is really the Lord of our lives — the Controller and Compass — we'll increasingly talk and walk like him.

When people ask *how* we become *like* Jesus, I say, "Read the New Testament."

When people demand more specificity, I say, "Read the Sermon on the Mount" (Matthew 5-7).

When people demand even more specificity, I say, "Well, Jesus said, 'Love the Lord your God with all your heart, and with all your soul, and with all your mind ... and ... love your neighbor as much as you love yourself.' He also said, 'Love each other just as much as I love you.' That means, of course, loving people invitationally, inclusively, and unconditionally. In short, it means loving people *to death*" (see Matthew 22:34-40; John 13:34-35).

When people demand a more concise response, I say, "Love God and be kind to one another."

Be Christian!

Every Shot I Ever Hit

Do this in remembrance of me.
— 1 Corinthians 11:24b

Two old friends were playing a round together. One of them was taking an especially long time to tee off — checking the wind, checking his grip, measuring the distance, changing his stance, fiddling around with the tee, looking up, looking down, looking all around, and then starting the routine all over again whenever distracted by a car, chirping bird, flowing stream, or his friend's breathing. Finally, his exasperated friend screamed, "What's taking so long? Just hit the dang ball, for cryin' out loud!" "But my wife is watching me from the clubhouse," the man explained, "and I want to make sure it's a perfect shot." His friend said, "Forget it! She's too far away! You'll never hit her from here!"

Golfers are like relatives who insist we endure those slides of their recent trip to Cleveland. Golfers remember every shot and every situation and assume we care.

Of course, the reason is every shot counts.

Nick Faldo has said it's not the quality of our good shots but the quality of our bad shots that determine good from bad scores.

Lee Trevino likes to say, "If you're not driving for show, you're not putting for dough."

Or as legend Bobby Jones assessed the situation, "It is nothing new or original to say that golf is played one stroke at a time. But it took me years to realize it."

I remember every shot I ever hit because they all counted in the final score.

John Freeman is a Methodist pastor who is currently a professor of practical theology at Emory University. He's also a golfer who sees the sport as a metaphor for exploring issues of faith and morality. In *Tee-ology: Golf's Lessons for Christians and Other Seekers* (1994), he commented on the strokes of golf and life:

In the strict economy of golf, each stroke counts exactly the same. It doesn't matter that athletically and aesthetically a 280 yard drive that carves the heart out of a narrow fairway bordered by hazards constitutes a far greater achievement than a six inch putt. On the scorecard — the same!

Some of the game's best known bromides root in this uncompromising reality. For example, "It's not how you drive but how you arrive."

He concluded: "Long or short, a stroke is a stroke. They all count the same, in faith as in golf."

A stroke is a stroke *in faith as in golf.* Everything we say and do expresses our faith. Strong. Weak. Mediocre.

Let me be more specific.

Everything we say and do is an expression of what we believe and what we believe determines our ultimate destiny. Every word and act and even thought add up to the final score. They all count.

Have our words (confession) exposed our faith as strong, weak, or mediocre?

Have our actions (conduct) exposed our faith as strong, weak, or mediocre?

Has our countenance (appearance or *how we look*) exposed our faith as strong, weak, or mediocre?

They all count in our relationship with the Lord. They all express what we know about him. They all express how much we remember him.

It's like Jesus said when he first instituted the sacrament of Holy Communion, "Do this in remembrance of me" (see 1 Corinthians 11:23ff.).

What do we remember when we gather around his table?

We remember his *invitational* love. He said, "Come to me, all you that are weary and carrying heavy burdens, and I will give you rest" (Matthew 11:28).

We remember his *inclusive* love.

He said, "For God so loved the world that he gave his only Son, so that everyone who believes in him may not perish but may have eternal life" (John 3:16).

We remember his *unconditional* love. He said, "Love your enemies ... If you love those who love you, what reward do you have?" (Matthew 5:43ff.).

We remember his *exemplary* love. He said, "Love each other just as much as I love you" (John 13:34, paraphrase).

We remember his *sacrificial* love. He said, "The Son of Man is going to be betrayed into human hands, and they will kill him, and on the third day he will be raised ... the Son of Man came not to be served but to serve, and to give his life a ransom for many" (see Matthew 17:22-23; 20:28).

We remember his *existential* love. He said, "I am with you always" (see Matthew 28:16ff).

We remember his *eternal* love.

He said, "I am the resurrection and the life. Those who believe in me, even though they die, will live, and everyone who lives and believes in me will never die" (see John 11:17ff.).

We remember God's love when we gather around the Lord's table.

I think of a story sent to me by Melissa Hinnbusch:

A soldier went home after serving in Vietnam.

He called his parents from San Francisco. "Mom and Dad," he said, "I'm coming home. But I have a favor to ask. I have a friend I'd like to bring home with me." "Sure," they replied, "we'd love to meet him."

But the son continued, "There's something you should know. He was hurt pretty badly in the fighting. He stepped on a land-mine and lost an arm and leg. He has nowhere else to go. I want him to live with us."

His parents said in unison, "We're sorry to hear that. Maybe we can help him find somewhere to live."

"No, Mom and Dad," the son insisted. "I want him to live with us."

"Son," said the father, "you don't know what you're asking. Someone with such a handicap would be a terrible burden on us. We have our own lives to live. We can't let something like this interfere with our lives. I think you should just come home and forget about this guy. He'll find a way to live on his own."

The son hung up the phone at that point.

The parents heard nothing from him from that point.

A few days after that last conversation with their son, they received a call from the San Francisco police. Their son had died after falling from a tall building. The police believed it was a suicide.

The grief-stricken parents flew to San Francisco and went to the city morgue to identify the body of their son. Immediately, they recognized his face. But with pain that seized the deepest recesses of their souls, they also discovered their son had lost an arm and a leg in Vietnam.

Unless we remember God's love when we gather around His table and internalize and incarnate that love in all of our relationships — invitational, inclusive, unconditional, exemplary, sacrificial, existential, and eternal — we'll never be pleased with the final score.

The hundredth anniversary of Norman Vincent Peale's birth was celebrated on May 31, 1998, by erecting a statue of him outside New York City's Marble Collegiate Church where he pastored for 52 years. Dr. Arthur Caliandro, Dr. Peale's successor who worked with Dr. Peale for eighteen years on Marble Collegiate Church's staff, offered this tribute:

"When we meet our Maker," Peale often used to say, "I think we're going to have to answer one big question: 'What did you do with what you were given?'" Without a doubt, Dr. Peale did the utmost with his gifts, both large and small. I was always touched by his sensitivity to people. Once he apologized to me four times in a day — four separate telephone calls — for a hurt that had been entirely unintentional. When a group of ministers asked him what the most important thing a pastor could do for his congregation was, he stated unequivocably, "Love them, love them, love them."

I think that's what the Beatles were trying to get across years ago when they sang, "All you need is love."

We have two services at Center every Sunday (8:30 and 11:00 a.m.).

The second service is fairly typical and fully loaded, including announcements, anthems, rites, children's sermons, and so on. It's exciting, joyful, and filled with fun, fellowship, and faith — just like a church should be!

The first service is low-key, quiet, meditative, almost monastic, and bare bones: hymns, Bible lessons, sermon, sacrament, and prayer.

While the content of both services is consistent — Christologically focused — the context or atmosphere is intentionally different to meet the different needs of people.

The first service always includes Holy Communion because the Bible and our confessions mandate it and because a lot of people like me need the sacrament more than quarterly.

The sacrament is observed by intinction during the first service (i.e., a piece of bread is dipped into the cup and then received into the spirit).

And every once in a while, some of the fruit of the vine symbolizing the blood of Jesus will drip from the cup or bread in the hands of the communicants onto my hands.

I think of two things when that happens.

First, I remember God bled and continues to bleed for us.

Second, I remember we are called to bleed for Him.

Dietrich Bonhoeffer explained it this way in *The Cost of Discipleship* (1937):

> *The cross is laid on every Christian ... When Christ calls a man, He bids him come and die. It may be a death like that of the first disciples who had to leave home and work to follow Him, or it may be a death like Luther's, who had to leave the monastery, and go out into the world. But it is the same death every time — death in Jesus Christ ... The wounds and scars ... are living tokens of the participation in the cross of his Lord.*

61

If we can remember every shot on the golf course or tennis court or bowling alley or baseball diamond or football field or wrestling mat or card game or whatever, we can remember every word, act, and appearance of our faith.

Unless we're being deposed or something, the truth is God gave us the gift of remembering who and what are important.

And everything we *are* is in remembrance of Him. Everything we *are* exposes our relationship with Him.

He remembers.

He said, "Then the righteous will answer him, 'Lord, when was it that we saw you hungry and gave you food, or thirsty ... or a stranger ... or naked ... or in prison?' " (see Matthew 25).

He remembers.

He is omniscient.

So let's take our best shot.

He will remember *forever.*

Apocalyptic Moments

The fruit of the Spirit is....   — Galatians 5:22-23

It's been said wisdom comes from experience and experience comes from messing up.

So I guess that means *the older the wiser* is another way of saying it's always easier to tell others the right way to do things after you've done them the wrong way for a long time.

Maybe that's why so many awful players become such good coaches.

Lee Trevino, however, isn't convinced. He has said he'd get a coach if he could find one who could beat him.

When I was in seminary, it was a cliché to say there's something at least a little strange about professors who've never been pastors telling prospective pastors how to do what they've never done.

I think of Dwight L. Moody who was criticized for *how* he *did* evangelism. Moody asked the inquisitor how he did it. When the man admitted he didn't do it, Moody remarked, "Well, I prefer the way I do it to the way you don't do it."

Fortunately, experience and education aren't the only paths to enlightenment. Sometimes the truth just seems to come to us out of nowhere. We *get it* without existential aid. I think of those times as apocalyptic moments. Believers chalk them up to divine inspiration.

One day it just hit me that I'm never going to qualify for the United States Open. It doesn't matter how much I practice or how many latest-technology weapons that I put in my arsenal. I'm never going to play on the Senior Tour. I'm never going to be the club champion at the course just off Route 19. I'm never going to be scratch.

It was an apocalyptic moment that reminded me of a paragraph from Kurt Vonnegut's *Palm Sunday* (1981):

*An Indianapolis cousin of mine, who was also a high
school classmate, did very badly at the University of
Michigan while I did badly at Cornell. His father asked
him what the trouble was, and he made what I consider
an admirable reply: "Don't you know, Father? I'm
dumb!" It was the truth.*

Everybody is important to God. But God doesn't make everybody capable of doing everything.

When I taught preaching at Kansas City's Nazarene Theological Seminary, I'd always open the first class with a quote from Karl Barth: "It doesn't matter whether one wants to preach. It matters whether one *can* preach."

It doesn't matter what we *want* to do. It matters what we *can* do.

The secret of personal fulfillment is finding out *who we are* and *what we're supposed to do* and embracing *ourselves*.

Because we tend to daydream too much and some folks around us tend to prescribe too much, it usually takes an apocalyptic moment to figure out who we are and what we're supposed to do.

One day it just hit me that my children don't really care what I think about who they are and what they're supposed to do. They have minds of their own. While I know they'll end up like most children who grow up to appreciate their parents, my word will come in second best when it comes to selecting a vocation, spouse, sport, and so on. Parents can only do their best and leave the rest to you know who.

In *How to Play Your Best Golf All The Time* (1953), Tommy Armour confirms my contention that golf is a metaphor for life: "When you miss a shot, never think of what you did wrong. Come up to the next shot thinking of what you must do right."

One day it just hit me that goes for husbands and wives too.

One day it just hit me that being a pastor isn't really about being *right about God* but rather *being right with God by doing right by people.*

Or as Paul described the conduct and countenance of people who have God in their hearts: "The fruit of the Spirit is love, joy, peace, patience, kindness, generosity, faithfulness, gentleness, and self-control" (Galatians 5:22-23).

One day it just hit me that being a believer is more about deeds than creeds. It's hard to figure that out on our own. That's why God's people have always depended upon apocalyptic moments or *revelation*.

By the way, it isn't necessary to hang out and wait for an out-of-nowhere apocalyptic moment. Just open the Bible. You'll be inspired and you'll also figure out if what you're believing and how you're behaving are more than auto-suggestion.

All I care to know is *love is the greatest expression of faith* — loving God by loving people; praying and working for the highest good for others regardless of who, what, where, or when without the expectation of being loved back.

All I care to know anymore is love is more important than my house, car, score, handicap, bank account, treasures, trinkets, trophy case, diplomas, degrees, and all of the other temporal things that will eventually end up in some church's rummage sale.

Only love will last: love for God — love for each other — love for others. Read the great commandment again (see Matthew 22:34-40).

And along the way, there will be many apocalyptic moments through which our Lord discloses the truth about living in and for Him.

While I know many Presbyterians are really obsessive about our Scottish heritage to the detriment of ethnic inclusion, I really had a woman in my first church ask me to baptize her Scottish terrier.

No, I didn't.

Yes, she went to another church.

Yes, *he did!*

I was asked at the last minute by a funeral director in New Jersey to preside at a funeral. Everybody looked so angry during the service. But people grieve in different ways. So I didn't give it much thought until I went to cash my honorarium and was told a stop had been placed on my check. When I called the funeral director to ask what I did wrong at the service, he said, "Bob, you didn't do anything wrong. I did. They stopped my check too. *They wanted a rabbi.*"

Two women came to tell me about the thousands of dollars of carpeting that they had ordered. "Great!" I said. "The church really needs it," I went on. Then I talked about God's house demanding our best stewardship. But as I spoke, the two women appeared excessively nervous. So I asked, "What's the matter?" "Well," they began, "we didn't know if the others would like the color or price that we liked. So we just went ahead and ordered it without talking to anybody."

And who said church board meetings had to be boring?

But my favorite moment occurred during my very first session meeting when I outlined the great plan of church growth. A long pause followed my presentation. Then an elder said, "You're crazy if you think we're going to do that."

Apocalyptic? I don't know. But it did set a tone for my ministry.

The truth is I don't like to talk about money. It seems to bring out the worst in people. For some reason which I cannot figure out from a spiritual perspective, many people have this crazy idea that they can give what's *left over* to God for the advancement of the Kingdom.

I remember hearing of a church which needed new carpeting. So the pastor was asked what he thought about it. "As you know," he said, "I'm called to address the spiritual problems of our church. Besides," he went on, "I forgot to take Carpeting 101 in seminary." Nobody laughed. A month passed and he was told: "We don't have enough money to buy new carpeting. What do you think about it?" "As you know," he repeated, "I'm called to address the spiritual problems of our church." Another month passed and he was told: "Pastor, we can't afford new carpeting. We can't even afford to pay your salary." *That caught his attention*! "Perhaps," he suggested, "we should talk about these problems at the next congregational meeting. But as you know, I'm called to address the spiritual problems of the church." After the pastor opened the congregational meeting with prayer, an elder stood and said: "Pastor, we've got a spiritual problem in our church. It's called bad stewardship."

That's why I don't like to talk about money. It reveals too much about our discipleship.

It's so apocalyptic.

Mind Your Manners

In everything do to others as you would have them do
to you.... — Matthew 7:12

Everybody's got pet peeves — annoying things that you'd correct or eliminate from the face of the earth if you were Director of the Universe.

While I'm particularly peeved by restaurants that charge extra for blue cheese dressing and refills and people who are fortunate enough to have just enough paper in the duplicating machine or staples in the stapler so they didn't even know they were empty when I showed up at 4 a.m. to use them and political partisans who like the odds of fooling all of the people some of the time and some of the people all of the time and courses like Augusta National which are harder to get into than heaven, there are two pet peeves at the top of my hit list.

Before I mention number two, I think it's important to mention that I've served as a police chaplain, highly esteem our law enforcement officers, and feel an especially close kinship with them because of my last name.

Though I know where real culpability ultimately resides (*avec moi*), I'm really peeved when I'm stopped for speeding on an open highway in the middle of nowhere. Being in the middle of nowhere, I don't succumb to the temptation to say things like, "Thank God there's no real crime in this area so you can ticket tourists in mini-vans and ruin a family's vacation before it starts," or "Your mom must be so proud." And when I'm asked if I know how fast I'm going, I've had to bite my lip to resist replying, "If I guess right, do I win a prize?"

I think of a story just sent to me by my son.

A state policeman stops a car puttering along at nineteen miles per hour. As he approaches the car to investigate, he notices five older women in the car. Obviously upset, the driver blurts out,

"Officer, I don't understand why you stopped us. I was doing exactly the speed limit. Why did you stop us?" Quickly figuring out the problem, the officer chuckles, "Ma'am, I'm not going to give you a ticket. I was just very concerned about your driving so slow on a major road. The nineteen you saw isn't the speed limit. It's the route number. You're on Route 19." Though a little embarrassed, the woman grins and thanks the officer for pointing out her mistake. But before she rolls up the window and moves on, the officer inquires, "Before you go, Ma'am, I've got to ask why the rest of the women in your car look so shaken and afraid. They haven't said a word since I stopped you." "Oh," the woman explained, "they'll be all right in a minute or two. We just got off Highway 119."

Then there's the story about an older woman in a big Cadillac about to pull into the last parking space in front of a busy store. But just as she is about to maneuver her big car into the parking space, two young tarts in a small convertible zip in, bounce out of their car, and announce, "That's how it's done when you're young and agile." Without hesitation, the woman smashes her Cadillac into the little sports car, backs up, smashes into it again, backs up, smashes into it again, and then rolls down her window and exclaims, "That's how it's done when you're old and rich."

I hope that's a good segue to my number one pet peeve: boorish behavior.

If there's anything I can't stand about myself as well as others it is a lack of manners. My director of the universe — my wife — refers to it as the absence of common courtesies.

There's a lot of wisdom framed and hanging in my study which says, "No kindness shown no matter how small is ever wasted."

Conversely, no unkindness shown no matter how small is ever harmless.

I am reminded of the Texan who was visiting Princeton University. He asked a young Ivy Leaguer, "Excuse me, boy, but where's the library at?" The bluenose replied, "I'm sorry, sir, but a Princeton man would never end a sentence with a preposition." "Sorry," the Texan proceeded, "but can you tell me where's the library at ... *jerk*!"

68

Jerk seems to be a good description for the kind of people in this world who aren't very kind, considerate, or Christian when it comes to others.

Jerks are manner*less*.

If golf is an appropriate metaphor for exploring the higher issues of life, it also exposes some of our baser instincts.

"Every golfer," Kathy Murphy stated in "Starter Set" (*Golf Journal*, July 1998), "should know and practice proper etiquette. That means knowing how to act so that other golfers can also enjoy the game and helping to respect the condition of the course."

Can you see the parallels?

Every person should know and practice proper etiquette. That means knowing how to act so others can also enjoy life.

Or as Jesus said, "In everything do to others as you would have them do to you" (Matthew 7:12).

As we've already noted, golf may do more to reveal than build character. The quickest way to check out somebody's attitude, ethics, and discipleship is one round of golf.

You learn a lot about somebody who always complains, curses, cheats, pounds and throws clubs, talks or hums or whistles or walks while you're putting, and generally shows no kindness or consideration for others because of her or his navel-gazing self-absorption.

It's like Fuzzy Zoeller observed: "I can't believe the actions of some of our top pros. They should have side jobs modeling for Pampers."

I was playing in a church outing several years ago on a little course just outside of Tarentum, Pennsylvania, called Woodlawn Golf Course. Number 5 at Woodlawn is a treacherous par four with hazards on the left and right and a landing area from the tee about the size of your average baptismal font. As I struggled to a *true six*, I watched one of our more notorious members chop his way up and over and around and through the hole. I counted at least eight hacks *before* he got to the green. After three-putting thanks to a self-awarded four-foot gimme, we walked to the next hole together. I turned to Eric our scorekeeper and said, "I had a six." The other guy who could teach Congress a lot about solving the deficit called out, "Me too!"

69

No wonder Paul Harvey commented, "Golf is a game in which you yell, 'Fore,' shoot six, and write down five." Or as Bruce Lansky lamented, "Golf has more rules than any other game, because golf has more cheaters than any other game."

I don't know how George Washington or Abe Lincoln or Jimmy Carter would have deported themselves but "Golf does strange things to people. It makes liars out of honest men, cheaters out of altruists, cowards out of brave men, and fools out of everybody" (Milton Gross).

While golf has worked for me as a positive therapeutic distraction as it teaches me a lot about myself, others, and many of life's issues, it's not for everybody. It brings out the worst in some people. And when that happens, it's time to consider alternatives.

It's like the old aphorism: *your cure is somebody else's curse.*

Everybody needs a therapeutic distraction.

Everybody needs a positive addiction.

That truth is a regular part of my pastoral care and counseling. I don't care what it is as long as it brings out a person's best. If it brings out anything less than a person's best, it's not positive or therapeutic and must be abandoned as the search resumes.

I'll never forget talking to Ralph Wrobley, a lawyer in Kansas City who was an especially good tennis player, about why he quit the sport. "When it became more work than play and evoked more anger than tranquillity," he confessed, "I knew it was time to quit."

So I've come up with two ways to determine if your current distraction is therapeutic and worth keeping.

First, does your game heal or hurt you?

Harold Mele is the most honest pastor in my experience. And I'll never forget the day that Harold, Eric, and I were playing nine holes at Vandegrift Golf Club in Vandegrift, Pennsylvania. After a particularly awful shot on the third hole, Harold just picked up his ball and walked off the course toward the clubhouse without a word. When Eric and I returned to the clubhouse about an hour later, Harold had breakfast waiting for us. He said, "I didn't want to spoil your game. It's more important to you guys. I just realized I don't really like golf all that much."

Then Harold went fishing. Golf wasn't for him.

It's not for everybody. But everybody needs something. Everybody needs a therapeutic distraction. My advice is to keep searching until you find the one that heals.

Second, does your game heal or hurt others?

One of my favorite stories is about a young boy who walked on a beach and saw a very old man preparing to catch crabs. The young boy had never seen anyone catch crabs before. So he sat in the sand and watched. The old crabber worked his strings and nets and soon began to catch lots of crabs. He threw them into a big bucket. It wasn't long before the little boy noticed crab legs inching over the top of the bucket. "Mister," the little boy said to the old crabber, "you better put a top on your bucket or all of your crabs are going to get away!" "Not a chance," the old crabber said to the little boy, "because whenever one of them gets to the top, the other crabs just pull it back down."

Aside from the fact that people don't want to play with crabs which is an excellent barometer of whether it's time to look for another game, you know you've *found your game* if your participation is for better than worse with your partners.

We could say that minding our manners is the best way to determine if we've found our game.

Does it heal or hurt us? Does it heal or hurt others? If it heals, we've found our game. If it hurts, it's time to give it up and take up another.

When it comes to golf, Abe Mitchell, the great British champion, was right, "The sum total of the rules of etiquette in golf is thoughtfulness."

That sounds a lot like the sum total of discipleship.

Jesus said, "In everything do to others as you would have them do to you."

Any game is worth keeping that treats us well. Any game is worth keeping that treats others well.

Our distractions cannot be divorced from our discipleship. All we are and all we do in all things at all times cannot be separated from who we are and what we are called to do as His.

That's why we must mind our manners.

God Knows!

You are the man!   — 2 Samuel 12:7

It has become fashionable to pretend a separation of private from public lives.

You know how it goes: "What I do in private is nobody's business ... Keep your nose out of my affairs! ... There's no connection between a person's private life and her or his profession ... What I do on my own time is of no concern of yours ... We're not a reincarnation of the Soviet Union! ... He's doing a good job! So leave him alone! Everybody deserves a private life!"

The assumption suggests it's possible to be publicly productive even if privately perverted.

Certainly, revelations from Pennsylvania Avenue have generated our recent obsession with the issue in an increasingly more seamy than serious way.

While tabloids, the tobacco industry, and *Saturday Night Live* are beneficiaries of this Gothic emission, I'm beginning to wonder if the pendulum is swinging too fast from the promiscuity of previous decades to a neo Puritanism. And as church, state, and fourth estate place the character of our *off*-White House residents under their seemingly self-righteous microscopes, I can almost hear the voice of reason and ultimate accountability asking rhetorically, "What's that I see in your eye?"

I can almost hear the only accountant who really matters cautioning us, "The measure you give will be the measure you get" (see Matthew 7).

As someone trying to be a Christian in all things at all times, I can never excuse behavior in others that insults God's holiness and cripples relationships. But that same Christianity compels me to acknowledge my own depravity as a context for judgment.

Indeed, ever since ostensibly faithful folks like King David of old and a couple of Jimmies of late made mockery of God's coded ethics established in Sinai, God's people have concentrated more

73

on the confession and repentance that redeem than the wages of sin. After all, that's why Jesus is called *Savior*. Or as he said, "God did not send his Son into the world to condemn the world, but to save the world through him" (see John 3).

Acknowledging sin and the escape of its ultimate consequences through confession and repentance should not be confused with license to be ethically irresponsible. I'm just being honest about who we are (sinners) and why we need Jesus (salvation from our sinful nature).

Sin is sin whether it's private or public. Privately concealed or publicly revealed, it's all the same to God. It insults His holiness and causes a breach only bridged by humility expressed through confession and repentance.

Though it has become fashionable to pretend a separation of private from public lives, whoever said Christianity is defined by political or public opinion? Conversely, Christianity is designed to lead the world as it is led by the Lord.

Putting it another way: our discipleship doesn't end when no one is looking. Putting it soberly: *everybody is looking!*

Everybody is looking at Washington and Christendom and all of the rest — *including you and me* — with enquiring minds.

That's why Christendom has never endorsed this ethical dualism pretending a disconnection between private and public lives.

That's why Christendom has always endorsed consistently connected discipleship, encouraging its adherents to love God privately and publicly through confession (talk), conduct (walk), and countenance (appearance) as taught in the Bible and exemplified in Jesus.

That's what it means to be *known* as completely Christian.

I was playing in a tennis doubles tournament many years ago in Kansas City. At a crucial moment in a closely contested match, I hit an ace right down the middle. It was perfect — right on the line with out-of-sight-out-of-reach pace. Immediately, the guy closest to the net yelled, "Out!" "Out?" I yelled back. But quickly, composing myself, conscious of congregants on adjacent courts and in the stands, I just bit my lip as my mind did a blue-flame burn. My partner turned around slowly and whispered matter-of-factly, "God knows!"

Yes, God knows.

God knew King David did the nasty with Bathsheba and tried to cover it up by having her husband knocked off on the battlefield.

God knew Judas sold out Jesus for cash and ideology.

God knew those two Jimmies looked spic-and-span in the sanctuary on the weekends but were as sin-stained as the gently gullible who were duped into emptying family coffers for their egocentric kingdom-building.

God knows what really happened in Washington.

God knows what's really happening on Main Street, USA.

God knows what's really happening behind closed doors.

God knows our true inclinations, motivations, temptations, and all the rest.

God knows when we cheat on Him.

God knows when we reject His will for our lives in public or private.

God knows our sinful attitudes and actions.

God knows all about us.

Our secret as well as seen lives are laid open before God.

God is, after all, *God. And He knows!*

That probably comes as a shock to people who think they can get away with bad stuff as long as it's out-of-sight.

When you've hit a ball deeply into the woods and nobody is within sight, it's easy to find the ball and have a good lie and clear shot to the green.

Or as Mickey Mantle said, "You know the old rule. He who have fastest cart never have to play bad lie."

Ain't it the truth?

Golf *like life* is so often about *lies*.

Bruce Lansky asked, "Did you ever stop and think why the pencils they give out with scorecards don't have erasers?"

When Harvey Penick, the late golf guru who gave us his little red and green books, was asked by some students if they could

75

improve their lies and play winter rules because of bad playing conditions, he replied, "Why don't you play golf?"

I've always liked this little anecdote from Mr. Penick:

> *Two proud parents came to me at the club and announced that their young son had just scored his first birdie.*
>
> *I agreed that was a wonderful event and asked them how long was the putt Junior made for the birdie.*
>
> *The parents said the putt was only two feet long, so they gave Junior a "gimme" to assure his first birdie.*
>
> *"I've got bad news for you," I said, "Junior still hasn't made his first birdie."*

I think of President Clinton who claimed to shoot 93 during the Bob Hope Chrysler Classic in Palm Desert, California (February 15, 1995). A spectator who followed him for all eighteen holes shook his head and reported, "You could erase the deficit overnight with addition like that."

No wonder former California Governor George Deukmejian noted, "The difference between golf and government is that in golf you can't improve your lie."

Unfortunately, folks always seem to be improving their *lies* in golf and life.

John Freeman was right in *Tee-ology: Golf's Lessons for Christians and Other Seekers* (1994):

> *It starts innocently enough, Discovering an unplayable lie, we kick the ball toward the fairway ... Or on the sly we take an extra "mulligan." Or we refuse to count the additional stroke for a lost ball because the rough, in our opinion, is not cut sufficiently. Or we disregard the out-of-bounds marker on account of our philosophical objection to unnatural hazards.*
>
> *Gradually, and probably imperceptibly, we grant ourselves a selective exemption from the rules of golf ... The one thing we improve in the process isn't our game, but the skill of rationalizing, going through the mental contortions necessary to justify our actions.*

76

Hitting it straight, Dr. Freeman concluded,

> *So maybe there is more at stake than we realize when we ponder whether to nudge the ball away from the bush or to dismiss the whiff as a practice swing. More insidious than our reducing our score or inflating our handicap is the real sin of building up our rationalizing muscle, making it harder to subdue on the job, with our family and friends, in our religious life.*

So how do we break the cycle of sin?

First, we must confess insulting God's holiness and hurting God, others, and ourselves in the process.

Second, we must repent and do the right thing.

Confession is mirror-mirror-on-the-wall-in-our-faces truth-telling. Confession isn't *spinning* the bad until it sounds *okay*. Confession is naked acknowledgment of how we have insulted God's holiness by our behavior and hurt God, others, and ourselves along the way.

When we cheat at golf, we break a few commandments, deprive others of fair competition, and delude ourselves about who we are and what we can do.

That's why my daddy doesn't allow mulligans, gimmes, winter rules, foot wedges, or anything else that improves our lies when we play. He often says, "If you don't count every shot and play by the rules, you'll never know how good you really are."

He's right!

That's why God expects — *Okay! Demands!* — repentance or *turning to the right.*

Confession and repentance please God so much. Or as the apostle says for God in 3 John 4: "I have no greater joy than this, to hear that my children are walking in the truth."

And the payoff is much bigger than an accurate accounting of our games and souls.

Listen to John's explanation (see 1 John 1:5-10 NIV): "If we claim to be without sin, we deceive ourselves and the truth is not in us. If we confess our sins, he is faithful and just and will forgive us our sins."

One of my favorite stories is about a preacher who visited a seasoned member of the church. As he sat on the couch, he spotted a large bowl of peanuts. "Do you mind if I have some?" he asked, "No, not at all," the woman replied. As the pastor got up to leave, he noticed he had emptied the bowl. "I'm terribly sorry, for eating all your peanuts," he confessed. "Oh, that's all right," the woman reassured him, "because ever since I lost my teeth, all I can do is suck the chocolate off them."

I guess we're kind of like those peanuts. We're naked before God. God knows all about us. And God's knowledge is not confined to our public appearances.

Fortunately, as we've already announced, we are sinners in the hands of a gracious God.

Or as R. C. Sproul explained (*The Holiness of God*, 1985):

> *A sound theology must be a theology where grace is central to it. When we understand the character of God, when we grasp something of His holiness, then we begin to understand the radical character of our sin and helplessness. Helpless sinners can only survive by grace. Our strength is futile in itself; we are spiritually impotent without the assistance of a merciful God. We may dislike giving our attention to God's wrath and justice, but until we incline ourselves to these aspects of God's nature, we will never appreciate what has been wrought for us by grace. Even Edward's sermon on sinners in God's hands was not designed to stress the flames of hell. The resounding accent falls not on the fiery pit but on the hands of the God who holds us and rescues us from it. The hands of God are gracious hands. They alone have the power to rescue us from certain destruction.*

We are blessed by our Lord whose knowledge of us may be surpassed only by His love for us.

That's good to know.

That's God.

Leave It On The Course

If someone does not know how to manage....
— 1 Timothy 3:5

My son and I just joined Indian Guides. Sponsored by the YMCA, it encourages dads and sons to be "Pals Forever" by providing opportunities and activities that build character and deepen family relationships.

We really like it!

One of the first big events is announcing your Indian name. Daniel picked "Golden Eagle" for himself and "Bald Eagle" for me.

At least he didn't name me "Water Buffalo Waistline."

Of course, that's not as bad as those school teachers and thirty-something moms who say to Daniel in my presence, "Isn't it nice that your grandpap could come with you?"

Then there's the oil change guy on Route 19 who keeps saying, "Your daughter brought in the van yesterday." I never confess being the father only of sons.

But the most recent greatest indignity occurred at a local restaurant when the waitress said I *look* like a clergyman. As someone who recalls the chap who said he would have become a pastor except for so many of them looking like undertakers, I was neither flattered nor amused.

And yet there's a line from Paul to Timothy that really tears at my soul: "If anyone does not know how to manage his own family, how can he take care of God's church?" (1 Timothy 3:5 NIV).

Ouch!

Over two decades in this business have taught me the strength of my ministry is inextricably dependent upon the strength of my family. While I've seen inept and ineffective pastors who have healthy families, I've never seen a pastor who wasn't strained, scarred, or stymied by a dysfunctional home.

The truth is healthy families foster healthy ministries. It's axiomatic. Show me a messed-up ministry and my guess is the etiology begins at the manse.

Obviously, the same goes for everybody else. Show me a messed-up world and my guess is fractured families are a very big part of the cause.

Healthy families breed healthy people. So if we're really interested in transforming church and society, there's no place like home to start.

Getting back to the church, a healthy church is the product of healthy church families and healthy church families are the product of healthy people.

Certainly, as a Christian pastor, I'm convinced personal health begins *after* Jesus is invited into the heart as saving Lord.

Lots of great things happen after conversion like invitational, inclusive, and unconditional love. That's *authentic* conversion. Anything less than praying and working for the highest good for others regardless of who, what, where, or when without the expectation of getting something in return isn't religion born of Christocentric conversion.

That's why the Imperials suggest as they sing, "There will never be any peace until God is seated at the conference table."

That's why I tell my non-Christian friends who are always calling my attention to conflicted churches, ill-tempered pastors, and irregular people, "Don't blame Jesus for some Christians!"

To put it another way, some Christians need some Jesus!

Or to borrow a few lines from G. K. Chesterton: "We have asked all the questions which can be asked. It is time we stopped looking for questions and started looking for answers ... The Christian faith has not been tried and found wanting. It has been found difficult and left untried."

Anyway, there are lots of problems in church and society. My guess — *belief* — is most of those problems could be solved by spending more time at home and fixing families. And every family could benefit from spending more time with somebody like Jesus who knows a lot about *saving*.

When I was preparing for ordination, The Reverend Harold F. Mante, my home pastor forever, gave lots of advice to me. He told me to love people *regardless*. He told me never to check the church's financial records because I'd start to look at people differently. He told me never to learn how to use office machinery. And he told me to play golf.

He was my pastor, wanted the best for me, and I've followed his advice throughout my ministry.

He advocated golf because he believed everybody needs something to get her or his mind off the problems of life and vocation. He could have said bowling, tennis, bridge, or something else because it is the intention not the vehicle that matters. Reverend Mante was counseling me to incorporate a therapeutic distraction or *mental bath* into my schedule in order to survive all of the above.

He played golf. He played golf with my dad. So he thought it was a good game for me. And he always said I would be able to leave my problems on the course.

God knows life can be tough.

I've got two close friends in ministry who are going through hell. I'm the pastor of a church that comes nowhere near its membership and mission potential. Every day isn't a hot fudge sundae for me. My son's football team can't seal the deal in big games. And sometimes I feel like taking down all of the smiley faces in my study before I throw up.

You know how I feel.

You know how I feel because you live in the same world.

Sometimes we completely relate to one of Dr. Addison Leitch's favorite comments: "You get all set to meet what life brings you, but it keeps coming at you left-handed."

Life can be so confusing and conflicted. That's why everybody needs a therapeutic distraction or mental bath.

We need to *leave it on the course.*

While the problems may not go away, we can always get back to them with a little more energy and a lot more perspective after recreation.

I think of a story from Martha Albertson:

Jerry is the kind of guy you love to hate. He is always in a good mood and always has something positive to say. When someone would ask him how he was doing, he would reply, "If I were any better, I would be twins!" He was a unique manager because he had several waiters who had followed him around from restaurant to restaurant. The reason the waiters followed Jerry was because of his attitude. He was a natural motivator. If an employee was having a bad day, Jerry was there telling the employee how to look on the positive side of the situation.

Seeing this style really made me curious. So one day I went up to Jerry and asked him, "I don't get it! You can't be a positive person all of the time. How do you do it?"

Jerry replied, "Each morning I wake up and say to myself, 'Jerry, you have two choices today. You can choose to be in a good mood or you can choose to be in a bad mood.' I choose to be in a good mood. Each time something bad happens, I can choose to be a victim or I can choose to learn from it. I choose to learn from it. Every time someone comes to me complaining, I can choose to accept their complaining or I can point out the positive side of life. I choose the positive side of life."

"Yeah, right! It's not that easy," I protested.

"Yes, it is," Jerry said. "Life is all about choices. When you cut away all the junk, every situation is a choice. You choose how you react to situations. You choose how people will affect your mood. You choose to be in a good mood or bad mood. The bottom line: it's your choice how you live life."

I reflected on what Jerry said. Soon thereafter, I left the restaurant industry to start my own business. We lost touch, but I often thought about him when I made a choice about life instead of reacting to it.

Several years later, I heard that Jerry did something you are never supposed to do in a restaurant business. He left the back door open one morning and was held up at gunpoint by three armed robbers. While trying to open the safe, his hand, shaking from nervousness, slipped off the combination. The robbers panicked and shot him. Luckily, Jerry was found relatively quickly and rushed to the local trauma center.

After eighteen hours of surgery and weeks on intensive care, Jerry was released from the hospital with fragments of the bullets still in his body.

I saw Jerry about six months after the accident. When I asked him how he was, he replied, "If I were any better, I'd be twins. Wanna see my scars?"

I declined to see his wounds, but did ask him what had gone through his mind as the robbery took place. "The first thing that went through my mind was that I should have locked the back door," Jerry replied. "Then, as I was lying on the floor, I remembered that I had two choices: I could choose to live or I could choose to die. I chose to live."

"Weren't you scared? Did you lose consciousness?" I asked.

Jerry continued, "The paramedics were great. They kept telling me I was going to be fine. But when they wheeled me into the emergency room and I saw the expressions on the faces of the doctors and nurses, I got really scared. In their eyes I read, 'He's a dead man.' I knew I needed to take action."

"What did you do?" I asked.

"Well, there was a big burly nurse shouting questions at me," said Jerry. "She asked if I was allergic to anything. 'Yes,' I replied. The doctors and nurses stopped working as they waited for the reply. I took a deep breath and yelled, 'Bullets!' Over their laughter, I told them, 'I am choosing to live. Operate on me as if I am alive, not dead.'"

Jerry lived thanks to the skills of his doctors, but also because of his amazing attitude. I learned from him that every day we have the choice to live fully. Attitude, after all, is everything.

And that's why I keep all of those smiley faces in my study.

That's why I play golf.

That's why I tell folks to find a therapeutic distraction and become addicted to it.

That's why I tell folks and often remind myself, "Leave it on the course!"

The problems don't go away. But when we're rested and renewed by our positive addictions, the problems don't put us away.

So leave it on the course!

Let me put it another way: *Go home*! Go home to God! Go home to your family! Take care of yourself!

You'll be glad you did!

And you just may find the smile on your face infecting the world around you!

A Positive Addiction

I am not ashamed of the gospel.... — Romans 1:16

We're looking for a new executive presbyter in Washington Presbytery. Our last one just took a job with the Synod of the Trinity as an interim associate executive of something or other.

Before you get too confused, a presbytery is kind of like a district (Methodist) or diocese (Roman Catholics). An executive presbyter is kind of like a district superintendent (Methodists) or bishop (Roman Catholics) except for respect and authority. Nobody knows what a synod is anymore. Actually, there's a movement to get rid of them. So I won't clutter your mind by trying to define what's soon to be deleted from our denominational dictionary. They'll probably be gone not long after we cross into the next millennium with or without the *parousia* which is why I'm glad our former EP's new job has a time-limited designation.

I really liked our last executive presbyter and I'm sad to see her go. I know she was inhibited in her ministry by some good old boys who long for the way things never were through scarcely veiled gender bias and a phobia about anything happening for the first time. And challenging the occupational wisdom of insuring success by following a boob, she took the mantle from a very popular and long-standing predecessor. But she was a decent pastor to pastors and their families. Personally, I cannot thank her enough for her care of my wife after a second miscarriage. She wasn't as perfect as her friends suggested but she was much better than her detractors pretended.

Of course, knowing the American Revolution was referred to as "The Presbyterian Rebellion" across the pond is a hint that we are almost impossible to lead. You've probably heard about the first group of Scots to hit shore building the First Presbyterian Church and the second group of Scots building the Second Presbyterian Church across the street. Proving ecumenism and even denominational unity to be a myth, it's not uncommon in many parts of America to find Presbyterian churches within spitting distance of each other. That's always the case where the Presbyterian population is dense.

That's a taste of the socioecclesiastical context awaiting our next executive presbyter.

Spanning the early and recent years of ministry, I've served on two successful executive presbyter committees (i.e., our choices lasted longer than your average pastorate). So here are my general qualifications for anyone crazy enough — *I mean called* — to take the job:

1. *Clearly Communicated Christology* — I expect our next executive presbyter to believe and behave like "Our vocation is to belong to Jesus" (Mother Teresa). It shouldn't be too much to expect our executive presbyter to mention Jesus by name more often than when closing prayers. I expect our executive presbyter to assess every aspect of life and ministry through a Christocentric filter. Jesus is, after all, the founder and focus of our faith. And as I tell our new members, if we agree on Jesus, everything else will eventually work out.

2. *Career Bureaucrats Need Not Apply* — Everybody knows our denomination is dying. So why would we be interested in someone schooled in keeping us headed in the wrong direction? We need someone who has been in the trenches, survived, succeeded, and empathetically knows what makes churches grow. Moreover, nobody in our local churches is going to listen to someone who tells us how to do what she or he has never done.

3. *Positive Pastoral Instincts* — Our executive presbyter must be a coach (encouraging people to be God's best for their lives and ministries) and referee (keeping people from hurting each other) rather than a ringmaster (one of those *my-way-or-the-highway* types). A short list of theological/ideological/idiosyncratic passions wouldn't hurt. If our executive presbyter cares too much about too many things, our presbytery will be as conflicted as churches with pastors who care about too many things. We need someone to enable, exhort, enlighten, and maybe electrify rather than condescendingly conspire to control us as a shill for the party line.

4. *Lover* — Our executive presbyter must enflesh our confession's *agape* love ethic: praying and working for the highest good for all regardless of who, what, where, or when without the expectation of getting something in return. As long as Jesus is Lord of all, *all* — left, right, middle and even confused — are important to the life of our presbytery. Indeed, I'd like our next executive presbyter to say, "You can be right about every area of theology and polity but wrong about Jesus and you're dead wrong and can lose your soul. You can be wrong about every area of theology and polity but right about Jesus and you will be saved."

Whoa! That looks like the job description for a pastor. So be it! We need a pastor to and *among* pastors.

But if you were to ask which qualification is the most important of all, I'd say our next executive presbyter must love Jesus *passionately*. Our next executive presbyter must be positively addicted to Jesus.

This should not strike any Christian as odd because a positive addiction to Jesus is the biggest part of the definition of being a Christian.

Every corner of the Kingdom requires its members to confess Jesus as *uniquely* Lord and Savior.

Every corner of the Kingdom requires its members to affirm questions like these: Do you trust in Jesus Christ? Do you intend to be his disciple? Do you intend to obey his word and show his love?

Every corner of the kingdom expects its members to be positively addicted to Jesus.

Again, I've always believed churches with members who really embrace Jesus as Lord and Savior don't have many problems.

Conversely, churches which are not positively addicted to Jesus have membership, education, financial, mission, and all kinds of relational problems. Churches without Jesus as the focus are always confused and conflicted.

When Jesus is not on the tip of our tongues, there's a bad taste in everybody's mouth.

Churches grow in every way when they say with positive addiction, "I am not ashamed of the gospel."

If you've been reading the preceding chapters and thought for one moment that I'm proposing golf as the solution to your problems, you've missed the point.

I believe golf or any other therapeutic distraction *enhances* life.

Jesus *is* life. That's why I pray and work for the church to grow. For when churches grow, that means people are coming alive emotionally, intellectually, spiritually, and eternally. Or as Jesus promised, "I am the bread of life" (John 6:48).

That's why I've always liked Mother Teresa's prayer:

> *Dear Jesus,*
> *Help us to spread your fragrance everywhere we go.*
> *Flood our souls with your spirit and life.*
> *Penetrate and possess our whole being so utterly that*
> *   our lives may only be a radiance of yours.*
> *Shine through us*
> *and be so in us*
> *that every soul we come in contact with may feel your*
> *   presence in our soul.*
> *Let them look up and see no longer us*
> *but only Jesus.*
> *Stay with us*
> *and then we shall begin to shine as you shine,*
> *so to shine as to be light to others.*
> *The light, O Jesus, will be all from you.*
> *None of it will be ours.*
> *It will be you shining on others through us.*
> *Let us thus praise you in the way you love best by*
> *   shining on those around us.*
> *Let us preach you without preaching*
> *   not by words, but by our example*
> *   by the catching force*
> *   the sympathetic influence of what we do*
> *   the evident fullness of the love our hearts bear to you.*
> *Amen.*

That's the enfleshment of saying, "Our vocation is to belong to Jesus."

Paul Azinger, the great golf champion who was diagnosed with cancer shortly after winning the 1993 PGA Championship, put it bluntly (*Zinger*, 1995):

> *People often ask me now, "Zinger, is golf still as important to you as it was before you had cancer?"*
> *Yes and no. Yes, of course, golf is important to me. I love the game; it is how I make my living. But no, golf is no longer at the top of my priority list. In fact, it runs a slow fourth. My priorities now are God, my family, my friends, and golf. Golf is no longer my god. Golf is hitting a little white ball. God is my God, and God is a whole lot bigger than golf.*
> *But don't get me wrong. I played some great golf at the end of 1994 and the beginning of 1995, and I plan on playing a lot more. You won't hear me out on the course, saying, "Woe is me. I missed that four-footer, but at least I'm alive."*
> *Oh, no. I'm playing to win. But then, in may ways, I have already won.*

Do you remember Richard Dortch? He was President of PTL. He was Jim and Tammy Bakker's right-hand man. Everybody knows the sad story of PTL by now. But few folks know about Richard Dortch. He was a respected superintendent of the Assemblies of God before joining the PTL team. Not long after becoming PTL's President, he got caught up in some of the negative addictions surrounding PTL which led to defrocking and imprisonment. By the grace of God, Richard Dortch repented and was restored to ministry by the Assemblies of God on November 20, 1991. He wrote about his experiences in *Integrity: How I Lost It, And My Journey Back* (1992).

Essentially, Richard Dortch confessed losing his integrity by failing to keep Jesus as the first priority or most positive addiction of his life and ministry. Instead of his personal relationship with Jesus controlling his behavior (the positive addiction), other people and commitments began to control his behavior (the negative addictions). He explained:

It wasn't until later, when the ministry came crashing down around me that I realized: Knowing God and being submissive to His will is more important than doing ... What God intends us to be is more important than what we do in life. That element is essential to living a life of integrity. Being is far more important than doing ...

When we fail, it is usually not the result of ignorance. Most of us know what we are supposed to do and the importance of why we should do it. When it comes to moral or spiritual failure, as Christians, we cannot plead ignorance ...

If I didn't fail because of ignorance, inability, or idleness, what caused my downfall? I think I know. I was too busy ... The secondary so absorbed us at PTL that we neglected the primary ...

At PTL we were often engaged in great, stressful, straining trivialities. While not sinister or malicious, these secondary priorities so absorbed us that we didn't have time left to do what God called us to do. We were involved in a thousand and one decent and wonderful programs and ministries, but while we were busy here and there, something of God slipped out of our lives. Our busyness kept us so preoccupied that we didn't have a keen interest in simply "knowing God" which should be every Christian's highest goal.

I learned a painful lesson: To maintain integrity I must put first things first.

When Jesus is the first priority or most positive addiction in our lives, our lives are better. When our personal relationship with Jesus controls our behavior, we are whole, happy, joyful, and secure. It's like he said: "If anyone is thirsty, let him come to me and drink. Whoever believes in me, as the scripture has said, streams of living water will flow from within him" (John 7:37-38 NIV).

Putting it another way: it's hard to become negatively addicted when we're positively addicted to Jesus. When we hang out with Jesus, it's hard to get into trouble. That's why Jesus is the most positive addiction. That's why Chuck Colson says, "I tell people, 'Don't follow me! Follow Jesus!' "

That's why Christian leaders follow the Leader and say: "If we meet and you forget me, you have lost nothing. But if you meet Jesus Christ and forget him, you have lost everything."

You may have heard about the aging parents whose son still lived with them. They decided to conduct a little test to discern their son's future. They put a ten-dollar bill, Bible, and bottle of whiskey on the kitchen table. They figured he would be a businessman if he took the money, a pastor if he took the Bible, and ne'er-do-well if he took the bottle. They left. When they returned to find their son had taken the money, Bible, and whiskey, they exclaimed in unison, "O Lord, help our son! He's going into politics!"

Or golf?

There are so many addictions out there. Some are good. Some are bad.

But there's only one addiction in the *real* church — *Jesus!*

That's why Mother Teresa counseled, "Let us free our minds from all that is not Jesus."

A positive addiction to Jesus is without existential or eternal liability.

A positive addiction to Jesus is existentially and eternally therapeutic.

So get hooked on him!

Holing Out

The time of my departure has come.

— 2 Timothy 4:6b

My dad holed the second ace of his half-century golf career on November 10, 1998.

He became a low single digit handicapper not too long after picking up the game as an Army drill sergeant at New Jersey's Fort Dix just after World War II.

Knowing perfectionist Ben Hogan had only one ace in his entire competitive career, a hole-in-one requires good providence — *luck* in the secular mind. But as my dad always counseled me about every sport, "The harder you work, the luckier you get."

Of course, I recall the apocryphal account of Moses playing with our Lord. Moses steps up to the first tee, blasts his drive right down the middle about 380 yards, and the ball rolls to the apron of the green. Our Lord steps up to the first tee, hits a worm-burner that rolls about 125 yards, a squirrel comes out of a tree just off the fairway and starts running with the ball in its mouth, an eagle swoops down and grabs the squirrel, lightning strikes the eagle as it begins to fly away, the eagle drops the squirrel on the green, and then the ball pops out of the squirrel's mouth and into the hole. Moses turns to Jesus and asks, "Did you come here to play golf or God?"

Anyway, my dad was a great athlete (football, baseball, swimming, etc., etc., etc.!) and remains a top amateur *for his age* in northeastern Pennsylvania. So I was really happy but not surprised at all when I got the news from my mom about the older man.

I haven't had a hole-in-one yet. I'm not *that* jealous or anything. It doesn't bother me *that* much that four members of the church have had aces in the last year. But I am thinking of stealing — *in a Christian kind of way* — James Dodson's (*Final Rounds*, 1996) idea and starting a Hole-in-None Society. I'm about to order a pub sign from the latest golf catalogue of useless accessories: "I

93

have never shot a hole-in-one and anxiously await the day I can give this sign to someone else."

Getting back to my dad: I used to hate losing to him, especially after I began to take the game seriously about halfway to octogenarian. We've had these grudge matches once or twice a year for a decade now. And I was obsessed with beating him.

I know that sounds rather odd for a non-competitive guy like me!

Unfortunately, I've turned the corner in the last few years. While I'm sure reading this will fire him up for future battles, I've got the edge now because I'm playing a little smarter and he's getting a little older.

That's why I say my victories are unfortunate. It means my dad is inching toward the final hole.

I'll never be ready for it.

My dad is the best man that I've ever met. He's always been faithful to God, wife, family, friends, country, and job. He doesn't understand the decline of faith and morality in church and society. He doesn't understand why our country increasingly sacrifices principles at the altar of a strong economy. He doesn't understand why people settle for less than their very best in all things at all times. He doesn't understand people who wait for other people to do what they should have done already. He doesn't understand egocentric people (i.e., *my* rights, *my* needs, *my* concerns, *my* feelings). He doesn't understand people who don't pray regularly, give generously, work hard, play harder, and love lavishly.

Eric Felack, a golf buddy who helped me lose to my dad and sister on many occasions, once commented after a bitter defeat that prompted some venting on my part, "You know, Bob, I'd give anything to play one more round with my dad. Enjoy him while you've got him!"

Aside from recognizing my sin and accepting Jesus into my heart as Lord and Savior, it remains the most sobering moment in my life.

Now I really don't care if I win or lose.

Okay, I'd rather win.

But I'm just happy to be playing with my dad.

I'm glad Eric woke me up before being forced to grieve with Mike and the Mechanics, "It's too late when we die to admit we don't see eye to eye."

And I'm glad you're reading this. Maybe you'll get it before it's too late. Just in case you've missed the point, here it is: "Love 'em while you've got 'em!" Someday everybody will return from the cemetery but you or me or them.

Before that final hole is played, take a cue from the Beatles: "Life is very short and there's no time for cursing and fighting."

God knows it will help the next time that you tee it up.

Everybody wants to hole out on a positive note. Everybody wants to finish well. It means a birdie or par or bogey or less than a snowman for golfers.

Holing out well for Christians is being able to say with Paul (2 Timothy 4:6b-8):

> *The time of my departure has come. I have fought the good fight, I have finished the race, I have kept the faith. From now on there is reserved for me the crown of righteousness, which the Lord, the righteous judge, will give me on that day, and not only to me but also to all who have longed for his appearing.*

I've reached the age when the days left aren't as many as the days spent. Maybe you know how I feel. Maybe you've reached the same conclusions about holing out:

1. Time runs out!

We don't have forever to live, learn, love, and get our jobs done.

We don't have forever to realize potential. We need to remind ourselves that the clock is ticking and we don't have forever to fulfill God's intentions for our lives.

2. Be the best that you can be in the time allotted to you!

God help any of us who say before holing out, "If I had my life to live over again, I'd ..." Doesn't that sound pathetic? Because you're reading it, you can avoid saying it!

Mother Teresa has some good advice on how to avoid such a tragedy:

At the end of life we will not be judged by
how many diplomas we have received
how much money we have made
how many great things we have done.

We will be judged by
"I was hungry and you gave me to eat
I was naked and you clothed me
I was homeless and you took me in."

Hungry not only for bread
– but hungry for love
Naked not only for clothing
– but naked of human dignity and respect
Homeless not only for want of a room of bricks
– but homeless because of rejection.

This is Christ in distressing disguise.

Becky Boyer, Center's Minister of Christian Education, likes to say, "One hundred years from now, it will not matter what kind of house I lived in, the kind of car I drove, or what my bank account was ... but that the world may be different because I made a difference in the life of a child."

Simply, don't be a *coulda, shoulda*, or *woulda* kind of Christian. *Be the best that you can be in the time allotted to you!* You'll be glad you did! The world will be better because of you! And you'll hole out with a smile on your soul!

3. You're going to live a lot longer with Jesus than anybody else!

You may have heard about the Unitarian minister in Michigan who set a record for preaching the longest sermon — 22 hours! Apparently, several folks stayed through the whole thing. According to the story, somebody yelled out at the end, "So what's the point of the sermon?"

So what's the point of living?

The Westminster Divines answered that years ago in *The Shorter Catechism* of 1647 (Question 1), "Our chief end is to glorify God, and to enjoy Him forever."

In other words, love Him and *live it up in Him!*

Paul E. Swedlund was one of my two closest friends in seminary along with Paul G. Watermulder. He fell off a mountain in Colorado on August 17, 1994, and went home to God.

Parenthetically — I always told him to play golf.

As Paul Watermulder and I went over our notes before Paul's memorial service at the McDonald's closest to Kansas City's Colonial Presbyterian Church, we said simultaneously, "I wonder who will do the next service?" I said, "I hope I go before you so somebody is around to say some nice things about me."

I'm old enough to know I'm not that important to too many people. Some folks pretend I matter. That's nice. But I know it's a short list of people who will lose sleep when the roll is called up yonder for me. I've often said if I were to die after preaching, there would be ham and cole slaw in fellowship hall on Wednesday and a congregational meeting to elect the next pulpit committee the following Sunday.

That's why I like these lines from Nicholas Sparks' *The Notebook* (1996):

> *My life? It isn't easy to explain. It has not been the rip-roaring spectacular I fancied it would be, but neither have I burrowed around with the gophers. I suppose it has most resembled a blue-chip stock: fairly stable, more ups than downs, and gradually trending upward over time. A good buy, a lucky buy, and I've learned that not everyone can say this about his life. But do not be misled. I am nothing special; of this I am sure. I am a common man with common thoughts, and I've led a common life. There are no monuments dedicated to me and my name will soon be forgotten, but I've loved another with all my heart and soul, and to me, this has always been enough.*

So when I die, I want people to say: "Bob Kopp loved Jesus. He loved his life and wife and boys and anybody who let him. And he loved people enough to point them to Jesus."

If that's true when I hole out, then I'll have done my best in the time allotted to me. I'll hole out with a smile on my soul.

Frank Dodson's *Final Rounds* is the recollection of a father and son's love for golf and each other that touches the deepest recesses of heart, soul, and mind. Specifically, it's about the final rounds of a father and son after learning the father had two months to live. So just like the preceding pages, it's not really about golf. It's about things that really matter.

The book ends with the son playing the Old Course at St. Andrews in Scotland where he had played a final round with his dad:

> *As we approached the Road Hole bunker on the seventeenth hole, I pulled a small blue velvet satchel out of my golf bag and began undoing the silken cords. The others watched solemnly ... I told them my old man had said golf is a game that made you smile ...*
>
> *As they smiled, I slowly scattered my father's cremated ashes around the Road Hole bunker and dumped some into the sand itself ...*
>
> *I walked slowly up the Scores, with a mind that was remarkably at ease for the first time in a very long time. Then I decided to walk back and just look at the Old Course in the darkness.*
>
> *Halfway down the hill, a boy passed headed the other way, a fellow late finisher. He was maybe eleven or twelve, hurrying home to dinner with his head bent and his bag on his back. He looked up as we passed, his clubs softly clicking. I thought of myself headed home from Green Valley. I thought of Jack maybe someday playing here with his old man.*
>
> *"Did you shoot a good one?" I asked.*
>
> *"Not so good, sir," he admitted. "Me driver's a wee bit off."*
>
> *"That's okay," I said. "Enjoy it. The game ends too soon, you know."*
>
> *"Right. Thanks."*
>
> *He walked on and I walked, and then I stopped. That's when I realized I'd heard it — my father's voice. I smiled.*

My *Father's* voice.

May all of us hear it and know *Him* before holing out.